AT THE EDGE

DARING ACTS IN DESPERATE TIMES

LARRY
VERSTRAETE

■SCHOLASTIC

New York   Toronto   London   Auckland
Sydney   Mexico City   New Delhi   Hong Kong

For my brother, Bob, and my sisters, Joan,
Maureen, Irene, and Janice

Text copyright © 2009 by Larry Verstraete.
Map p. 142 by Paul Heersink/Paperglyphs. Copyright © 2009 by Scholastic Canada Ltd.

First published by Scholastic Canada Ltd. in 2009.

ISBN 978-0-545-27335-0

12 11 10 9 8 7 6 5 4 3 2 1   10 11 12 13 14

Printed in the U.S.A.   40
First American edition, September 2010
Cover design by Steve Scott

TABLE OF CONTENTS

INTRODUCTION

A man sees a stranger fall off a subway platform into the path of an oncoming train. . . . A boy's village is destroyed, his family dead or missing, and now soldiers are looking for him. . . . A tsunami bears down on a woman and her two young children — there is no way they can survive if they all stay together. What do they do? What choices do they have?

When people face overwhelming situations, they must make critical decisions. The path, though, is not always clear. The choices may be confusing, the risks high, the consequences uncertain. Stay or flee? Resist or submit? Help another or save yourself?

This book contains stories about people who were forced to the edge. It is about their actions, and about the choices they made in difficult situations. Reading their stories "from the outside," we might be tempted to judge each one: Yes, that was a good choice or No, that wasn't. We could label that person fearless, this one strong, that one less so. But perhaps we should ask questions of ourselves, too. Caught in the same desperate situation, with the clock ticking relentlessly, the stakes just as high, what would *I* do?

CHAPTER 1

AT THE EDGE OF DISASTER

The reputation of a thousand years may be determined by the conduct of one hour.

— JAPANESE PROVERB

Evacuate immediately, Vincent Coleman was told. But he couldn't. Not yet, anyway.

FINAL MESSAGE

Flames shot into the air and oily black smoke billowed into the morning sky over the Halifax, Nova Scotia, harbor on December 6, 1917. A ship was on fire at Pier 6, a couple of hundred yards away from the Richmond train station where Vincent Coleman worked as a dispatcher.

Railway dispatcher Vincent Coleman.

Minutes earlier, at precisely 8:45 A.M., there had been a collision in the harbor. A Belgian relief ship, *Imo*, had plowed into the starboard bow of a French ship called the *Mont-Blanc*. The *Mont-Blanc* had caught fire. Her terrified crew launched the lifeboats and fled in panic, abandoning the vessel. The unmanned ship drifted, burning all the while, until finally it came to rest against Pier 6. Within moments flames had spread to the wooden dock. While a tugboat strained to pull the crippled ship away from the pier, firefighters worked feverishly to extinguish the blaze from the shore.

From nearby Richmond station, Vincent Coleman kept a watchful eye on the smoke and flames as hundreds of curious spectators gathered — men heading to work, women running errands, children setting off to school, soldiers on leave, and sailors awaiting duty.

The crew of the *Mont-Blanc* knew the real threat. The ship carried munitions bound for Europe, where World War I was raging. Stored in crates and drums on board was more than 2,590 tons of explosive materials — wet and dry picric acid, gun cotton, benzol, and TNT.

As flames multiplied, sailors from the *Mont-Blanc* tried to spread word along the dock — *Danger . . . Explosion . . . Run!* Their warnings went unheeded. The crew spoke French, not English, and hardly anyone understood the message.

But the harbor staff that regulated traffic along the waterfront also knew of the *Mont-Blanc*'s cargo.

Messengers were dispatched to warn shopkeepers and workers to evacuate immediately.

At the Richmond station Vincent heard the message. He had to leave right away. That was the order he'd been given. But as he turned to flee, Vincent remembered. A passenger train from Boston was coming. It was due to arrive at the Richmond station in minutes. No one aboard knew of the danger, of the fire spreading along the dock, of the explosives on the ship. They were heading straight for the disaster. Vincent had a decision to make: go now and get as far away as he could, or turn back and send a final message to the coming train.

Stop trains. Munition ship on fire. Making for Pier 6. Goodbye boys.

Ignoring the evacuation order, Vincent turned back to the station. There was no time to waste. He quickly tapped out a message on the telegraph, a warning in the dots and dashes of Morse code: STOP TRAINS. MUNITION SHIP ON FIRE. MAKING FOR PIER 6. GOODBYE BOYS.

Moments later, around 9:05 A.M., the *Mont-Blanc* exploded. It was the largest man-made explosion in history up until that time. The force of it was staggering, so powerful that the ship's steel hull was shredded into fragments. Part of the *Mont-Blanc*'s anchor was pitched more than 2 miles; a cannon barrel flew 4 miles in the opposite direction. Shards of twisted metal shot into the sky and fell like molten bullets around the harbor. A cloud of smoke 20,000 feet high mushroomed over Halifax.

The blast ripped apart buildings, touched off fires, and smashed windows. It fired glass and splintered wood across the city. Churches, houses, schools, and factories collapsed. A huge clock was blown out of a tower in Truro, 60 miles away.

The force of the explosion caused a massive tsunami in the harbor. As debris and oily soot rained down

Thousands of homes, like this one, were smashed to kindling.

on Halifax, the wave rose and washed over buildings, tearing houses from foundations and ripping bricks from mortar. Those who had survived the initial explosion scrambled for cover and clung to anything found floating in the water.

More than fifteen hundred people died in the explosion. A further nine thousand were injured. Many were onlookers who had gathered to watch the fire. The explosion devastated the industrial end of the city, flattening almost every building within a mile of the blast center. Gone in an instant were rail lines, telephone lines, telegraph cables, and water and electricity mains.

The Richmond station collapsed into a heap of broken rubble. Vincent Coleman was one of the casualties. The warning message he had sent moments before the explosion was his final act. Because of his action, hundreds of lives were saved. His message arrived in time to halt the incoming passenger train from Boston, as well as other trains bound for Halifax.

Vincent's message, along with others sent later by railway officials, was passed from station to station, and helped spread word of the disaster far and wide. Alerted to the tragedy, the railway reacted quickly, pouring medical aid and relief into the stricken area. As a result, many lives that might have been lost were saved.

Although we will never know why Vincent chose to do what he did, his valiant act has not been forgotten. In Halifax a street near his old home now bears the

The *Imo* after the explosion.

name Vincent Street in his honor, and in the Maritime Museum of the Atlantic a number of his personal objects are on display. These include the pocket watch that was found with his body, the telegraph key he used to send the message, and his wallet, which still holds the raffle tickets he bought a few days before the explosion.

If Stanislav Petrov pressed the button, there would be no turning back. It would be the start of a third world war — a nuclear holocaust.

COUNTERSTRIKE

Lieutenant Colonel Stanislav Petrov sat in the commander's chair in the glass-walled room of Serpukhov-15, a secret bunker just outside Moscow. It was a few minutes past midnight, and the beginning of his shift.

The room, as always, was a hive of quiet activity. Serpukhov-15 monitored American nuclear missile positions. It was filled with military officers and engineers glued to computer screens that spewed information gathered by satellites and radar stations across the Soviet Union. On this night, Stanislav was the head of its operations. It was not his normal position. He was a software engineer, but twice a month he took over the command post.

It was 1983 and the world's two superpowers — the United States and the Soviet Union — were at a standoff. Each had a stockpile of nuclear weapons ready to use with the press of a button. Stanislav's mission that night was clear: He was to monitor American activities, detect any incoming missiles, and, if the United States attacked, order an immediate counterattack.

That night, though, all was normal in Serpukhov-15. The computers hummed quietly, their screens a soft glow of reassuring information. There was nothing to worry about . . . for the moment.

Then at 12:14 A.M. Stanislav's computer screen turned bright red. "An alarm went off. It was piercing, loud enough to raise a dead man from his grave," he said.

The screen showed that an American missile had been launched. It was heading their way.

Both the Soviet Union and the United States built up a supply of missiles during the Cold War, a period of tension between the two countries that lasted from the end of World War II until the early 1990s.

Stanislav knew what he had to do. In fact, he had written the procedure manual himself. In the event of a nuclear attack by the United States, he was to press a red button labeled START. This would launch Soviet nuclear missiles, allowing them to strike back and hit the United States in an all-out nuclear counterattack before the Soviet Union's capacity to retaliate was completely disabled.

All eyes turned to Stanislav. He hesitated. The computer system, he knew, was riddled with flaws. There had been questions about its reliability before. Was this just a false alarm? There was no way to tell.

The computer screen flickered and changed. A second American missile had been launched from the same base, it indicated. Then it showed a third missile, a fourth, a fifth.

Alarms rang. Lights flashed. The START button blinked. Stanislav had to act immediately. If the United States had launched missiles, they would arrive in fifteen minutes. If Stanislav waited longer, it would be too late to do anything at all.

Still he hesitated. Something didn't seem right. "I just couldn't believe that just like that, all of a sudden, someone would hurl five missiles at us. Five missiles wouldn't wipe us out. The U.S. had not five, but a thousand missiles in battle readiness."

There was a second reason Stanislav hesitated. It was something that he thought of every time he commanded this post. If he pressed the button, there would be no turning back. It would be the start of a third world war, a nuclear holocaust. Could he live with himself, knowing that?

Tension mounted. Seconds seemed to stretch into hours. Then Stanislav grabbed the phone and placed an urgent call. He knew that with five incoming missiles showing on the screen, his superiors would have automatically been alerted to the danger. They'd be reviewing their war plans, preparing to strike.

"False alarm," he told them.

But was it really? Stanislav was relying on gut instinct, not hard evidence. "I understood I was taking a big risk," he said.

Nervous minutes passed. No missiles arrived. There was no nuclear destruction.

The computer system had erred.

Relief began to settle over the room, followed by pats on the back, smiles all around, and congratulations to Stanislav for making the right call.

Although he was a hero to the people in the room that morning, Stanislav Petrov had crossed a fine line. He had disobeyed orders and acted on his own. Instead of pushing the button, he'd bypassed the rules. In the Communist-run Soviet Union, where rules governed almost every facet of life, and those who disobeyed suffered severe penalties, Stanislav's act was akin to mutiny. An inquiry was launched, and rather than

Each side feared a "first strike" that would disable them before they could strike back with their own nuclear missiles.

commending Stanislav for his bravery and quick thinking, authorities hushed the incident to keep it a secret.

Exhausted from the stress of the investigation, Stanislav retired from the army and lived in poverty on a small pension, his story largely unknown. When the Soviet Union crumbled and was replaced by a freer, more democratic government in 1991, his story became public.

On May 21, 2004, Stanislav Petrov received a long overdue honor. The San Francisco–based Association of

Stanislav Petrov as a young officer.

World Citizens gave him its World Citizen Award in recognition of the role he had played in preventing a global catastrophe. In 2008 a documentary film, *The Red Button and the Man Who Saved the World*, was released worldwide, drawing even more attention to a hero who, until then, had largely been unknown.

> *"I just believed in my judgment and experience and I trusted those around me."*
>
> — STANISLAV PETROV

Someone had to fly over the smoldering reactor. Anatoly Grischenko was just the man.

SMOTHERING CHERNOBYL

Anatoly Grischenko sat in the pilot's seat of the Soviet-made helicopter beside Gourgen Karapetian, his close friend. The two were top-notch civilian pilots, among the finest in the Soviet Union.

Below them they could see the smoldering ruins of Reactor No. 4 — twisted metal, chunks of concrete, and molten graphite. Barely two weeks earlier Reactor No. 4 had stood tall and proud. But that was before the explosion at the nuclear power plant in Chernobyl, Ukraine.

It had started with a simple safety check. Reactor No. 4 was powered down, then restarted. It was standard protocol. But on start-up that day there was an unexpected power surge. The nuclear reaction went wild, steam pressure built, and the core overheated. At 1:23 A.M. on April 26, 1986, the reactor exploded.

Instantly the 10-foot-thick concrete and steel shield blasted to bits and 50 tons of radioactive uranium turned to vapor. Clumps of lethal material landed around the reactor, starting more than thirty fires. Alarms sounded and thirty-seven fire crews arrived to try to extinguish the flames. With little protection from radiation they fought the fire through the night. By 6:35 A.M. the flames on the roof were out, but the fire within the reactor continued to burn, spewing a constant stream of radiation into the atmosphere.

At first the Soviet Union downplayed Chernobyl, but as days passed people were evacuated from nearby towns. Radiation spread around the globe and countries in Europe noted abnormally high levels in the air. It became impossible to hide the truth. Chernobyl was a man-made disaster, the worst the world had ever seen.

The Soviet Union considered its options, and came up with a bold plan to absorb the radiation: bury the reactor under tons of sand, clay, and other material dropped from helicopters dragging buckets on 700-foot lines. Dozens of trips were made, the mound of dumped material grew, but still radiation oozed from the molten shell of Reactor No. 4. Forced to come up with another plan, experts suggested an even bolder move: They would use concrete to encase the reactor in a tomb.

To be successful, precise optical measurements had to be taken. Someone with know-how and a steady hand had to fly over the reactor and swoop in close to gather data. Anatoly Grischenko and Gourgen Karapetian were perfect choices—experienced commercial test

The remains of a damaged reactor at the Chernobyl nuclear plant seen from a helicopter just days after the fire was extinguished.

pilots with reputations of being able to handle tough situations with calm and ease.

Anatoly and Gourgen voluntarily accepted the mission. To steer around smokestacks of other reactors, dodge plumes of smoke, hover for just a few moments, and then slip away quickly took nerves of steel and an understanding of updrafts that comes only with experience.

It also meant being exposed to radiation. In large uncontrolled doses, or even smaller ones accumulated over time, radiation can be like poison to the body, capable of killing cells, altering organs, and spawning cancer. Sometimes the effects aren't felt for weeks, months, or even longer.

To safeguard the pilots from radiation, a lead shield was installed in the floor of the helicopter cockpit. With their trust in the shield, Anatoly and Gourgen

Over a thousand vehicles used to control the disaster were abandoned afterward because of the high level of radioactivity they contained.

made their first flight. They steered as close to the reactor as possible, taking measurements quickly, then banking to escape the "hot zone," the most concentrated region of radiation. When a dosimeter, an instrument that registers radiation levels, showed that radiation inside the cockpit was three hundred thousand times more than normal, they knew that the shield was virtually useless.

Still they flew again. At first it was to gather more measurements. Later it was to help with the delicate job of hauling buckets of wet concrete to the site. It was a task described by some as "like dropping a weight at the end of a string from a skyscraper into a teacup."

For a month the two pilots flew into the danger zone almost every other day. On at least five occasions Anatoly flew directly over the reactor itself. And although Gourgen was sometimes ill, Anatoly felt none of the side effects associated with radiation poisoning — headaches, nausea, vomiting, hair loss. Anatoly knew he was lucky.

After a few months at home Anatoly was again called back to Chernobyl. His special piloting skills were needed to fly 15-ton sections of a ventilation system to the damaged reactor. To fly over the reactor again, to expose his body to further radiation, meant that he would likely add to any damage that might have already been done.

Anatoly knew he would be putting himself in yet

more danger, but once again he accepted the mission. Over the next month he transported cargo to Chernobyl, flying near the still-active reactor many times and on three occasions directly over the hot zone itself. In his diary he wrote, "I have flown more dangerous flights at Chernobyl than in all my twenty years as a test pilot."

In September Anatoly returned home to Moscow. The work of entombing Chernobyl was almost finished and he was looking forward to a quieter life. He felt tired, but shrugged it off as normal.

A visit to the doctor, however, suggested something far different. Tests showed that his white blood cell count was low. It was the first of many signs that all was not right inside his body. Soon there were others — bouts of nausea and diarrhea, persistent coughs, reddened eyes. His voice disappeared entirely. Anatoly was diagnosed with leucopenia — cancer. The cause, his doctors said, was "unknown."

But Anatoly knew the cause — Chernobyl. All those flights over the reactor, the constant exposure to radiation. That was the reason, he was sure of it.

Doctors assured him that was not the case. "This is an illness from inside you. You had it before Chernobyl," one told him.

In the months that followed, Anatoly's condition worsened. He felt he was fighting two losing battles. One was against the disease itself. The other was against doctors and government authorities who refused to admit that Chernobyl might have been the cause of his illness. Anatoly felt that they were shirking responsibility, covering up the mess that Chernobyl had become, and abandoning not just him, but also thousands of others who had fought Chernobyl and were now suffering radiation-related diseases.

"This is an illness from inside you. You had it before Chernobyl."

As Anatoly's condition deteriorated, his wife, Galina, and his friend Gourgen took up his fight. Galina wrote a passionate letter to Soviet leader Mikhail Gorbachev. Gourgen, meanwhile, worked political and medical channels both at home and abroad. Gradually the government acknowledged some responsibility. Slowly the full story of Chernobyl became public.

Despite the support of friends and family, and rounds of medical treatment—including a bone marrow transplant in the United States—Anatoly died of cancer in July 1990.

Anatoly Grischenko has been recognized with a number of awards posthumously, including the Flight Safety Foundation Heroism Award, and the Hero of the Soviet Union, one of the country's highest honors.

CALLED TO ACTION | October 3, 1986 / North Atlantic Ocean

Soviet nuclear submarine *K-219* was on a routine mission when a sudden explosion rocked one of the missile tubes, killing three sailors. Power lines shorted out and the automatic controls that regulated the nuclear reactor jammed. Without controls, the sub's nuclear reactor ran continuously, steadily building heat and higher levels of radiation. The threat of a nuclear meltdown was real — if the reactor exploded it would cripple or sink the submarine and pour poisonous radioactive elements into the ocean and atmosphere.

For twenty minutes seaman Sergei Preminin struggled with the jammed operating mechanism inside the missile compartment. Radiation levels were dangerously high, so the hatch doors were locked to keep radiation from leaking to the rest of the submarine. It was sweltering hot inside the damaged compartment. Eventually Sergei brought the reactor under control, but when he turned to leave, he found the high pressure buildup inside the compartment had made the hatch door impossible to open. From the outside, crew members tried feverishly to open the door. But, overcome by heat exhaustion, Sergei died in the compartment. Today, there is a monument to him in the town of Krasavino, Russia, with these words engraved on it: *To Russian Seaman Sergei A. Preminin, who prevented the world from a nuclear catastrophe.*

Jillian Searle couldn't stay above water — not with both children.

LETTING GO

The morning after Christmas Day, 2004, the sky over Phuket, Thailand, was a brilliant blue. The wind was soft and inviting, the temperature warm and even. For the Searle family, who had traveled from Australia to Phuket on vacation, it was a perfect day. Bradley, Jillian, and their two blond-haired boys, Lachie and Blake, opted to have breakfast by the hotel pool.

Moments after Bradley left to get a diaper from their room for Blake, Jillian heard a roar coming from the beach. It sounded like distant thunder, a rumble that was growing louder by the second.

"I turned around and I just saw masses, masses of water coming for us," she said.

Unknown to the Searles, or to hundreds of thousands of other people in Thailand, Sri Lanka, India, and other countries that ringed the Indian Ocean, a massive earthquake had ripped across the ocean floor hours earlier, sending shock waves through the water and unleashing a giant tsunami.

Jillian grabbed her sons and tried to outrun the wave, but it was too swift and too huge. The wall of water crashed over them, its force so great that it ripped clothes off Jillian's body. But she didn't notice. She was clinging to her children, paddling madly, desperately trying to stay above water.

As she grew weaker, Jillian's situation became more serious. It was impossible to stay afloat with both children. "I had both of them in my hands — one in each arm — and we started going under. I knew that if I held on to both, we would all die."

She had to let go of one of her sons. But which one? Letting go would be like issuing a death sentence.

An earthquake under the seafloor in the Indian Ocean caused the giant waves of the 2004 tsunami.

Jillian chose the older of the two. Lachie, at five, had a better chance of survival than the twenty-month-old baby. "Someone take my son!" she begged. But Lachie clung to his mother, pleading with her not to let go. He couldn't swim and was terrified of the water.

"I could feel him squeezing me. And he said to me, 'Don't let go of me, Mummy.' But I knew I had to," Jillian said.

Alyce Morgan, a seventeen-year-old Australian girl on vacation with her family, spotted Jillian trying to keep the two boys alive. She reached out and grabbed on to Lachie. As the current tore them apart, Jillian glanced back at her son. "I remember looking back at my five-year-old boy thinking that this will probably be the last time I will see him alive."

From the hotel balcony Bradley watched helplessly as the wave rolled over the beach. The force of the water slammed the hotel doors shut, making them impossible to push open. There was no way to reach his family.

Finally, after prying open the doors, Bradley was able to leave the hotel. He reached the beach just as a second wave of water came crashing in. After the wave had subsided, he searched the grounds for his missing family. He found Jillian and Blake clinging to playground equipment. They were safe, but Lachie was missing.

"I remember looking back at my five-year-old boy thinking that this will probably be the last time I will see him alive."

"You have to find him because I let go of him," Jillian cried to her husband. "I gave him to somebody else, and I let go of him. . . . There is no possible way I can live my life knowing that I took his hand off mine."

Together they combed the beach and searched the hotel, calling out Lachie's name. The devastation was widespread and horrific. Everywhere there were dead and injured, heaps of debris, and people like them, searching for missing loved ones.

When at last Jillian spotted Alyce her hopes soared, then just as quickly fell. Alyce had struggled to climb on top of a bar counter while at the same time keeping Lachie's head above water, but the force of the wave had torn Lachie from her hands. He'd been lost to the tsunami.

Still they searched. Lachie could have survived, they told themselves. It *was* possible. But after two hours, even that slim hope began to fade. How could a boy so young, alone and unable to swim, survive such destruction? Jillian prepared herself for the worst. "I was screaming, trying to find him, and we thought he was dead."

Then, covered in mud and clutching the hand of a

Thai security guard, there was Lachie. He was alive, uninjured. Their reunion was joyful, filled with hugs and grateful tears.

In the hours that followed, Lachie's survival story slowly emerged. After he'd lost his grip on Alyce, he'd stayed afloat by dog-paddling as fast as possible. Then, as the water rushed over him, he'd grabbed on to a door handle and managed to keep his head just above water.

"I cried for Mum for a long time, and then I was quiet," he told his father.

Anxious to return home, the Searles caught the first possible flight out of Thailand. Life, they knew, was too precious to waste with regrets.

The Searles family back home in Australia shortly after the tsunami. From left to right: Blake, Bradley, Lachie, and Jillian.

"We are just so lucky to walk away with the small children I have got. One of who[m] can't even swim and is petrified of water—even the pool at home—and one who is a little baby. I just can't believe they are still here."

— JILLIAN SEARLE

Six-year-old Deamonte Love meant to keep his promise, no matter what the cost.

TAKING CHARGE

In the aftermath of Hurricane Katrina, Deamonte Love was spotted clutching his baby brother in one arm. With his other hand, he led a toddler with braids who, in turn, was holding hands with a string of four other children. All seven were lost, separated from their parents by wind and water, and wandering down a Louisiana city street. Deamonte had made a promise to look after the others, and he meant to keep it.

Hurricane Katrina started as a tropical storm in the Bahamas, but on Saturday, August 27, 2005, as it began weaving across the Gulf of Mexico, it was upgraded in status. Forecasters predicted the hurricane, packing high winds and massive waves, would hit Mississippi and Louisiana hard.

Orders to evacuate the low-lying city of New Orleans were issued. Thousands obeyed, anxious to flee before the storm wreaked havoc. For those who couldn't leave—or wouldn't—emergency centers were established. Of these, the Louisiana Superdome was the largest.

In Catrina Williams's apartment building, many

people stayed to face the storm. With her two children, Deamonte and five-month-old Darynael, plus relatives and neighbors, she braced for what was to come.

On Monday, August 29, Hurricane Katrina made landfall, walloping Louisiana with 140-mile-per-hour winds. Catrina Williams could hear the storm outside, the wind howling, far-flung debris pounding the walls, rain pelting the windows. She gathered her children close and prayed that it would soon be over.

At the Superdome, the wind tore two holes in the roof, striking fear in the thirty thousand people inside.

Flooded New Orleans streets following Hurricane Katrina.

Finally Katrina swirled north. As it passed over land, the hurricane lost some of its fight. Winds diminished. Clouds emptied themselves of rain. To residents in northern states, Katrina was nothing worse than a bad summer storm.

In New Orleans the hurricane had pushed water inland, filling to capacity the levee system that protected the city from floods. On Tuesday, August 30, two levees failed. Then, one after another, other breaches followed. Water gushed down streets, broke through soggy walls, and poured into homes. Soon 80 percent of the city was flooded. In some sections, the water was 20 feet deep. The people of New Orleans, already exhausted by days of fighting the storm, now faced far worse.

Catrina Williams, her children, and other residents of their apartment building were trapped. With rivers of water flowing down streets, there was no easy escape. The storm had cut their power. There was no light, no air conditioning, no clean running water. They waited in the sweltering dark, their food supplies dwindling. Without a working refrigerator, the food that was left began to spoil. Soon there was no milk, even for the baby.

The city was in chaos. The death toll climbed steadily. Overwhelmed by confusion and panic, emergency crews struggled to cope. Shelters were filled to capacity, hospitals bursting at the seams. There were desperate

A rescue helicopter arrives to evacuate people forced to
leave their New Orleans homes for shelters in other states.

people everywhere, some seriously injured, others
wading the flooded streets dazed and confused. Many,
like Catrina Williams, were trapped in apartment blocks
or homes. Boats and helicopters were dispatched to rescue them.

On Thursday, September 1 — four days after the hurricane first bore down on New Orleans — a rescue

helicopter finally arrived at Catrina Williams's building. There were dozens of residents to take away, but only one chopper and not enough room for everyone. Send the children first, the helicopter crew told the residents. We'll be back in twenty-five minutes for the others.

Over the *chop-chop-chop* of whirring blades the parents discussed their options. Who should go? Who should stay and wait for the helicopter to return?

With only seconds to decide, Catrina Williams weighed her options. Was this the only choice? Wasn't there some other way? If they followed this plan, her children, along with the others, would be airlifted to safety first; the adults would stay in the flooded building to wait for the helicopter's return. At six years old, her son Deamonte would be the oldest child in the group.

Catrina Williams made her decision. As she lifted her son onto a helicopter destined for safety, she made him promise he would look after the others. "We did what we had to do for our kids because we love them," Catrina Williams would say later.

The helicopter would be back in minutes. They would soon be together with their children again.

As the chopper doors closed and the helicopter whisked away, Catrina Williams and the four other mothers cried, consoled each other, and waited. The helicopter would be back in minutes. They would soon be together with their children again.

But the helicopter did not return. Somehow in the confusion, with pressing emergencies all around, the helicopter dropped the children off, then flew to a different destination. The residents of the apartment block waited, counting down the time. Worry turned to panic as twenty-five minutes . . . an hour . . . then two hours ticked by. Would the helicopter ever return? Would they see their children again?

The children were dropped off at an evacuation point in the city of Baton Rouge, Louisiana, to join others who had been rescued from their homes. No one noticed them. They were just faces in the ever-growing crowd. Separated from their rescuers and left to themselves, the children were lost and alone, but Deamonte knew what to do. He would do as he had promised his mom, and take charge. He took his baby brother and his cousins by the hand. Together they formed a human chain, a string of seven small children wandering down Causeway Boulevard looking for their parents, too afraid or shy to ask for help from strangers.

At the apartment building, another helicopter finally arrived to rescue Catrina Williams and the others. They were brought to an emergency shelter in San Antonio, Texas, not knowing the children had been dropped off somewhere else. They searched the sea of faces there, begged busy workers for information, and scoured bulletin boards splattered with photos of those missing or found. Their search turned up empty. The children were not there.

Over 400 miles away in Baton Rouge, someone finally took notice of Deamonte and the others. Even in the chaos it was odd to see them alone. Where are your parents? Who are you? What happened? they were asked.

They were taken to an evacuation center, checked by paramedics, fed, and given clothes and toys. Slowly, as the children relaxed, as their trust in the rescuers grew, they spilled the story a little at a time. Deamonte told them his father was tall, his mother short. He gave his address, phone number, and the name of his school. Pictures were taken of the children and posted on a website for missing persons that had been set up for the survivors of Hurricane Katrina. A search began for their parents, but with the death toll mounting and almost one hundred thousand people trying to trace family members, the chances of locating them were slim.

Far away Catrina Williams hung on to hope and kept the search going. On Saturday, three days after her children disappeared, she checked the website, found photos of them there, and with the other mothers wept with joy and relief, their prayers at last answered. Their children were alive.

The next day, Deamonte and the other children were put aboard a private plane and flown to San Antonio to be reunited with their parents. While she waited for the plane to arrive, Catrina Williams struggled to put into words what she was feeling. "All I know is that I just want to see my kids," she told reporters. "Everything else will just fall into place."

CALLED TO ACTION | **September 11, 2001 / New York, U.S.A.**

On the morning of the terrorist attacks on the United States, Rick Rescorla, vice president for corporate security at a large brokerage firm, was in his corner office on the 44th floor of Building Two of the World Trade Center. When the first plane slammed into Building One at 8:48 A.M., Rick was told by a Port Authority official to keep everyone at their desks. Rick defied the order. "Everything above where that plane hit is going to collapse," he argued. "The overweight will take the rest of the building with it. And Building One could take out Building Two."

Every few months, Rick had conducted evacuation exercises to prepare workers in case a real emergency ever happened. Immediately he grabbed a bullhorn, barked orders, and put into place the well-practiced drill. He ordered the evacuation of Building Five across the plaza where one thousand of his fellow employees worked, and then led another twenty-seven hundred employees in Building Two down crowded stairways, clearing floors as he went. Along the way, he sang songs to bolster morale, used humor to offset tension, and gave assistance to those who needed it.

By the time the second plane hit Building Two at 9:07 A.M., most of his employees were already outside, and the rest were well on their way. But three were missing. Rick and two assistants voluntarily went back to look for them. When last seen shortly before the tower collapsed, Rick was on the tenth floor, still searching for stragglers.

Of the thirty-seven hundred Morgan Stanley employees in the World Trade Center, six died that day. Rick Rescorla, the hero who ensured the safety of thousands, was one of them.

CHAPTER 2

AT THE EDGE
OF TERROR

You gain strength, courage, and confidence
by every experience in which you really
stop to look fear in the face.

— ELEANOR ROOSEVELT,

ACTIVIST AND FORMER U.S. FIRST LADY

The polar bear ripped apart the tent and mauled the campers inside. Armed with only a pocket knife, what chance did Eric Fortier have?

JUST IN CASE

In Nunavut, in Canada's far north, the sun never quite sets in summer. Night just becomes a hazier version of day, so when a polar bear attacked their campsite at 3 o'clock in the morning, Eric Fortier could see it plainly as it pinned his friend, Alain Parenteau, to the ground and raked him with its razor-sharp claws.

Standing nearby, helpless and screaming, was Patricia Doyon, Alain's girlfriend. Their tent was in tatters and Alain was faceup, kicking at the bear. His T-shirt was drenched in blood. Behind Eric, watching and screaming, too, was his own girlfriend, Anne Dumouchel.

The four friends from Gatineau, Quebec, had been canoeing the Soper River for a week, edging closer to Soper Lake, where they would be airlifted out. By day they took in the sights as they paddled. At night they pitched two tents side by side, relaxed in each other's company, and soaked up the Arctic charm.

An avid camper and canoeist, Eric slept with a pocket-knife by his side, a long-standing habit of his. On this trip, the knife was just a precaution. Eric's research had told him that there weren't supposed to be polar bears in Soper Valley. And they hadn't seen a single bear—not until now, on the last night of their trip as they camped on the shore of the lake, just 5 miles from their pickup spot.

The polar bear had sneaked up on them while they were asleep. It had sniffed around the tents, nudged Eric's and Anne's, and then taken a swipe at it, waking

Polar bears are the largest land predators. A large male polar bear can weigh up to 1,500 pounds.

them both and sending them into a screaming frenzy. In seconds the bear had moved on to the second tent, reduced it to tatters and attacked Alain.

Seeing his friend pinned under the bear, Eric looked for a way to distract the animal and give Alain a chance to escape. A large stone had been tied to the corner of his tent to stabilize it. Eric slashed the cord with the pocketknife, grabbed the stone, and heaved it at the bear. It broadsided the bear, bounced off its thick fur, and startled it just long enough for Alain to creep away.

The bear charged Patricia next. She ran, slipping on bedrock, with the bear at her heels. Then she fell. The bear was on top of her in moments.

"Roll into a ball!" Anne screamed at her.

Patricia did, curling up to shield herself as best she could.

Turning and running away was not an option.

Eric fired more rocks at the bear, distracting it long enough for Patricia to scramble to her feet. But the bear smacked her down and mauled her back, shredding her clothes and tearing her skin. She screamed in terror and pain.

Turning and running away was not an option. Seeing Alain hurt and now Patricia, too, Eric knew he had to act. Clenching the handle of his pocketknife, the 4-inch blade extended, Eric ran toward the bear. The bear didn't see his approach. Eric aimed for its head. It didn't even flinch when Eric jabbed the knife into the fur at its jaw. Eric jabbed again, then once more. He felt the blade hit bone, and it came out covered in blood. This time the bear noticed. It ceased its attack on Patricia, gave a shrug, and lumbered away.

Eric watched the bear amble off, then turned to his friends. All was quiet. Alain was bleeding from wounds to his head, neck, side, and thigh. His face was drained of color and he was in shock. Patricia was crying, her clothes torn and her back bloodied. Both required

The closest human settlement for help was Kimmirut, a remote fishing hamlet on Baffin Island, Nunavut.

medical attention, but the closest place they might get help was on the other side of the lake at the Inuit community of Kimmirut, population four hundred.

Within minutes they were in the canoes, cargo stowed in careless heaps around them. About 20 feet from shore, they stopped and considered their plan. The bear, an excellent swimmer, might be nearby—perhaps even stalking them. It would be best to stay together, safer and faster to paddle as a team rather than apart. They strapped the canoes side to side into a single unit.

Alain was in rough shape, pale and shivering, his eyes vacant. To keep Alain conscious, Eric and Anne spoke to him and prodded him for answers.

Eric and Anne paddled, digging into the water with urgent strokes, buoyed by the knowledge that they were getting closer to Kimmirut. They would find help there— a doctor or nurse—someone with medical training.

When they finally reached shore Eric ran 2 miles to town, while Anne stayed with Alain and Patricia. It was 6:30 A.M. when Eric arrived—three hours since the polar bear attack. The streets were deserted, the health center locked. Frantically he pounded on neighborhood doors and, when one finally opened, poured out his story.

Someone alerted the Royal Canadian Mounted Police. Soon Eric was in a pickup truck, a nurse by his side, heading back down the dirt road to the others. Minutes later Alain and Patricia were being taken back to

Kimmirut. From there they were airlifted to the hospital in Iqaluit, Nunavut's capital. Stitches took care of most of the wounds, and after a short hospital stay both Alain and Patricia were sent home.

On December 9, 2002, the four friends gathered together in the ballroom of Rideau Hall, the Ottawa residence of the governor-general of Canada, Her Excellency the Right Honourable Adrienne Clarkson. While Anne, Alain, and Patricia watched, Eric Fortier was called forward.

"You did what was brave," the Governor General told Eric as she awarded him the Medal of Bravery. "You did what was right."

> *"When you see your friends getting hurt, you have to do something."*
>
> — ERIC FORTIER

Bound and gagged in the basement of the house, seven-year-old Erica Pratt desperately looked for a way to outsmart her kidnappers.

ERICA'S NIGHTMARE

Erica Pratt's nightmare began one Monday evening while she was walking with her five-year-old sister, Naliyah, along a well-traveled street in Philadelphia, not more than a stone's throw from where they lived with their grandmother.

A battered white car suddenly pulled alongside the girls.

"Erica, come here," a man called.

Erica refused, but before she knew it the car door had swung open. The driver, an overweight man in a white T-shirt, stepped out and seized her. She kicked and screamed, but the man overpowered her. Erica was hauled to the car, grabbed by its passenger, and pulled inside. Naliyah watched, too horrified to move. Within seconds the car had sped away, leaving Naliyah alone on street.

Erica was gone.

Naliyah ran, tears running down her cheeks. "They took her from me, they took her from me!" she cried over and over.

Strangers came and tried to comfort Naliyah. Between sobs, she told the story. The news spread to Erica's grandmother, Barbara Pratt, then to Erica's mother, Serina Gillis, and finally to the police.

Erica had been kidnapped—snatched off the street by two strangers.

Eventually the car pulled up to a two-story house with a sagging porch and peeling paint, about 10 miles away from the kidnapping site. Erica was dragged inside and down to the dingy basement. Silver duct tape was wrapped around her head to cover her eyes and used to bind her thin wrists and ankles.

The two men delivered a chilling warning. They told Erica they would kill her if her grandmother didn't give them money. Then they left, leaving Erica tied up tight on a thin mattress in the basement of the dark and filthy house.

Barbara Pratt received a telephone call just twenty minutes after Erica's kidnapping. Then she received another, and still another as Monday night melted into Tuesday morning. Each call delivered the same message: Give us $150,000 or you'll never see Erica alive again.

Neighbors quickly organized themselves and walked the streets of the neighborhood looking for the missing girl. The police and FBI started their own search. They combed the streets, questioned residents, and checked scores of leads, most of which turned out to be dead ends. By Tuesday a total of $10,000 in donations had been raised for information leading to the arrest of the kidnappers.

As the hours passed, two questions crept into people's minds. Where was Erica? Was she still alive?

In her corner of the basement, Erica waited. Up above she could hear the creak of the men's footsteps as they moved across the floor. After a time the house grew quiet and still. Had the men left? Erica could only hope.

The kidnappers had provided Erica with very little. A plastic bucket to use for a toilet. A bag of potato chips if she got hungry. Some juice if she became thirsty. The night ticked slowly away.

Outside, the summer sun rose, turning the air hot and muggy. Inside the dank basement though, with tape wrapped around her eyes, Erica knew only darkness and a growing sense of urgency. She knew the men would return. They had threatened to kill her, and she had no reason to doubt they would do it. She had to act. But what could she possibly do? Her eyes were covered, her feet and hands bound, and she had nothing to help her escape.

Perhaps there was a way Erica could help herself.

Erica pondered her predicament. Perhaps there was a way she could help herself. She began to gnaw at the tape that bound her wrists. It took some time, but eventually Erica chewed right through. Once her hands were free, she tore off the tape around her eyes and feet. In the darkness of the basement she eventually found the stairs and felt her way up to the kitchen.

Erica headed to the front door. Freedom was on the other side. She turned the knob, but the door was locked and wouldn't budge, no matter how hard she tried. She was so close to escaping, just the thickness of a door away.

Through the living room window Erica looked out to the street. People were out there, walking, riding their bikes, busy with their lives. Here was the help she needed.

She smashed the glass, tore at the window screen, and yelled with all her might. "Help me! Won't you help me? I'm stuck in this house!"

On the street two teenagers were chatting. It was almost 8 P.M. on Tuesday evening, close to twenty-four hours since Erica Pratt had been kidnapped on the other side of town. The teens heard her desperate cry coming from the dilapidated house. They looked and saw a tiny figure in the window. A small girl, screaming for help.

With some tugging and squeezing, they pulled Erica out through the window.

"Thank you. Thank you," Erica said, over and over.

Then Erica told the story of the two men who had taken her, of the hours spent inside the house, of the mother and grandmother she was anxious to see.

The teenagers flagged down a police car, and Erica was rushed to the hospital to be checked out.

Notified by police, her grandmother and mother met her there, relieved to find her alive and well. Other than some tape still stuck in her hair, and slight damage to her eye from the binding around her head, Erica was in good shape.

Based on Erica's description of the kidnappers, two men were arrested and charged. They had chosen Erica as a target based on rumors circulating in the neighborhood that Erica's grandmother had come into a fortune.

But the kidnappers' plan to hold Erica ransom had been foiled by Erica herself.

Erica Pratt is carried by her uncle after her release.

Cool composure got thirteen-year-old Clay Moore out of a life-threatening jam. Clay and a group of friends were skateboarding at a school bus stop when a man in a red truck pulled up. Wielding a gun, the man forced Clay into the vehicle. As the truck sped away, Clay secretly removed a safety pin holding a tear in the sleeve of his jacket and slipped it into his mouth. "I thought it would be helpful," he explained later.

When they reached a wooded area, the truck pulled over. The kidnapper pulled Clay out, bound his wrists and feet with duct tape, and stuffed a sock in his mouth and taped it shut. Then he left. When all was quiet, Clay used his tongue to push the sock against the tape on his mouth. In time the tape came undone and the sock and safety pin tumbled to the ground. With a stick held in his mouth, Clay pushed the pin closer to him. When it was within reach, he picked it up with his teeth and dropped it into his hands. Using the pin, he cut through the tape and freed himself. Then he walked out of the woods. When he spotted a farm worker on a tractor, he used the man's cell phone to call his mother. Police speculate that the kidnapper intended to hold Clay for ransom, but Clay's actions hindered the kidnapper's plans.

The mountain beckoned Andrew Brash, but so did something else. Something more important. A man's life.

CLIMBING EVEREST'S GRAVEYARD

On Mount Everest — the world's highest mountain — the air is thin, lacking in oxygen. In many ways this is its greatest hazard. The human body reacts negatively to oxygen deprivation: energy evaporates, muscles stiffen, the brain swells. Death is a real possibility. Especially in the "Death Zone."

The Death Zone is the uppermost region of Everest, the part of the mountain above 26,000 feet where oxygen is most wanting, climbing is most dangerous, and death often strikes. Because rescue helicopters cannot operate at extreme altitudes, and carrying bodies down the mountain is risky, the dead are usually left behind — frozen reminders of Everest's danger.

On Friday, May 26, 2006, Andrew Brash, a thirty-six-year-old teacher from Calgary, Alberta, was in the

Death Zone. It was the final leg of a long climb up the northeast face of Everest, a journey Andrew had spent months preparing for and years dreaming about. With Andrew were three other men. They were part of an expedition that was being led by Dan Mazur, a forty-five-year-old from Olympia, Washington.

Andrew had sacrificed a lot to get this far: careful scrimping and saving to fund the journey; making numerous phone calls and sending e-mails to secure a spot on the expedition team; years of training on lesser mountains to gain the experience he needed. He had

Within reach: Andrew Brash's video shot of the summit of Mount Everest from base camp.

even taken out a life insurance policy to protect his wife and young family—just in case.

The men left their base camp 2,000 feet below the summit around midnight. Their plan to climb the day before had been thwarted by lightning storms, vicious winds, and whirling snow. But that night Everest was calm, the air still, and the sky clear. Bundled in warm clothes, equipped with a radio, headlamps, and bottles of oxygen, and strengthened by weeks of training on the lower reaches of the mountain, they were confident they would reach the summit. If their luck held they would be back at base camp by afternoon, when the weather on Everest often shifted and turned sour.

Just before reaching the First Step—a steep sloping ledge, one of two major obstacles climbers had to pass on the way to the top—death made a sudden appearance. Along the trail they came across the body of David Sharp, an English climber who had died ten days earlier.

"I had a sick feeling in my stomach as I prepared to walk by David's body," Andrew wrote later.

Andrew and the others didn't know at the time that David Sharp's death had caused great controversy around the world. Sharp had died making a solo attempt on the mountain. At least forty other climbers had passed him on the day of his death. A few tried to help, giving him oxygen and encouragement, but most simply ignored his plight. Intent on reaching the summit, they had passed by, leaving him to die alone on Everest.

The act was condemned by many, but news of the controversy hadn't reached Andrew and the others. Holed up for weeks at various base camps on the mountain, far removed from the buzz of the media, they knew only that David Sharp had died in the Death Zone, and that, like more than two hundred other unfortunate climbers, his body had been left on Everest.

The team pushed on. By the time they reached the narrow ledges and steep climbing ladder at the Second Step — the last hurdle on the way up — the sun was beginning to rise above the horizon. The summit was not far off, just 780 feet away, well within reach. Then once again the Death Zone surprised them.

Andrew noticed that expedition leader Dan and their guide from Nepal, Jangbu Sherpa, had pulled off the trail. They were speaking to someone. Who could it possibly be?

"Can you tell me your name?" he heard Dan ask.

A weak voice answered, shaky and confused. "Yeah! Yes! I know my name. My name is Lincoln Hall."

Andrew recognized the name. Lincoln Hall was a well-known Australian climber. What was he doing alone on Everest?

Despite the severe cold, Lincoln was only partly dressed. He was sitting upright, no hat on his head, no gloves on his hands, his feet dangling over the edge of a 10,000-foot drop. His orange suit was unzipped to the waist and his fingers were frozen white. He was shivering uncontrollably and there was a glazed expression in his eyes. Lincoln didn't seem to be carrying any supplies, and when he spoke it was slowly, the words slurred and jumbled. He was close to death. It was just a matter of time.

"I imagine you're surprised to see me here," he mumbled.

While the men tended to fifty-year-old Lincoln, Dan pulled out the radio and made a call to base camp, alerting others to their discovery. Slowly Lincoln's story emerged. On his way down the mountain the day before, he'd run into trouble. His brain swollen from lack of

Andrew Brash's photo of Lincoln Hall (foreground) as the climbing team found him, delirious and perched on the edge of the mountain.

oxygen, he'd collapsed in a coma in the snow. His team-mates had tried to help, but after nine hours reached a difficult decision. They'd been in the Death Zone far too long. To stay any longer meant putting their own lives in peril. Lincoln was beyond saving, essentially dead already, they figured. So they collected his back-pack, oxygen, food, and water, and left Lincoln not far from the body of another climber who'd died just hours before. That night, the expedition leader phoned Australia to break the sad news to his family: Lincoln's not coming back.

But miraculously Lincoln *had* survived the night. Somehow he'd picked himself up and fumbled through the darkness, delirious and close to death.

The base camp crew told Dan that help was on its way. Rescuers would be carrying oxygen, warm clothes, medicine, a stretcher — everything needed to take Lincoln Hall safely down the mountain.

Andrew knew it would be hours before rescuers reached them. They were so close to the summit now, just within sight of their goal. He could almost taste vic-tory. If they stayed with Lincoln, it might be too late to continue the climb.

The men considered their options. They could escort Lincoln down the mountain, meet rescuers partway, and then continue the climb. But Lincoln was frost-bitten, suffering from hypothermia, and too weak and wobbly on his feet to take more than a few steps. The idea was quickly abandoned.

Having the team split up, one or more of the men staying with Lincoln while the rest climbed to the summit, was briefly considered as well.

Although the mountain beckoned Andrew, so, too, did something else, something more important. A man's life was at stake. Lincoln Hall's team had given him up for dead. Andrew couldn't do that. Neither could the others.

"I said no to the idea," Andrew explained later. "I felt that we had come this far as a team and that we should stick together through this as well."

Lincoln Hall's team had given him up for dead. Andrew couldn't do that. Neither could the others.

In the end the men decided to wait together with Lincoln, doing what they could to help him until rescuers arrived. They gave him food, tea, and oxygen. They sheltered him from the elements and, just as importantly, protected Lincoln from himself. He stumbled to his feet several times, teetering dangerously close to the edge. Three times they tackled him, pinning him down. Finally they tied him with a climbing rope. It was the only way to make sure he didn't topple off the mountain.

"I hope he survives," Andrew said to the others at one point.

"Yeah, so do I," said Lincoln, who'd been listening.

Slowly Lincoln's condition improved. Around 11:30 A.M., after almost four hours, help arrived. Lincoln was carried down the mountain to safety, severely frostbitten and weary, but alive.

For Andrew and the others, though, it was too late to resume the climb. There was no way they could make it to the summit and back to base camp before dark. They had been in the Death Zone for too long already; they would have to descend the mountain. Reluctantly they turned around.

That moment came with mixed feelings for Andrew: satisfaction knowing that he'd helped save a life; anger at Lincoln's team for abandoning him in the first place; frustration at coming so close to his goal, then having to give it all up.

The news of Lincoln Hall's rescue traveled around the world. David Sharp had died just days before, passed by climbers too intent on reaching the summit of Everest to stop and help. Now here was the story of four climbers who had made a different decision, who had abandoned their own climb and given up the chance of a lifetime to save a fellow climber. To the world, the men were heroes.

For Andrew Brash the story continued. In 2008 he returned to Everest and made the difficult climb to the summit, fulfilling at last his lifelong dream of conquering the world's tallest mountain.

> *"On many occasions we've been called heroes. I can't tell you how undeserved this feels. I realize that in helping Lincoln and taking the course of action we did, we helped to save his life, but the things I felt afterwards — the frustration and depression — have at times left me feeling like a fraud."*
>
> — ANDREW BRASH, *EXPLORE*,
> SEPTEMBER/OCTOBER 2006

CALLED TO ACTION | **September 24, 1988 / Busan, South Korea**

At the halfway point in the Finn class sailing event at the 1988 Summer Olympic Games, Canadian athlete Lawrence Lemieux was in second place, despite the 13-foot-high waves and dangerous 35-knot winds. In limited visibility and treacherous conditions, it took all of Lawrence's skill to stay on course and ahead of the competition.

With the finish line in sight, something else caught his eye — to his right a boat from another race had overturned and was being tossed by the waves. Two sailors from the Singapore team were in the water. One was clinging to the capsized boat. The other was being swept away by the current. He would soon be lost at sea.

There was no time to signal for help. "The first rule of sailing is, you see someone in trouble, you help him," Lawrence explained.

Abandoning the race, Lawrence steered his one-person vessel downwind, cutting across steep waves to reach Joseph Chan, the man in the water. Lawrence pulled Joseph aboard his vessel and headed to Shaw Her Siew, the man clinging to the capsized boat. Then he waited with them for help to arrive.

Afterward, Lawrence continued the race, knowing full well that it was too late to regain his lead. He finished in twenty-first place, but in an unusual move the Olympic Committee granted him a

CALLED TO ACTION | **September 24, 1988 / Busan, South Korea**

second-place finish — his position just before abandoning the race to save the stranded sailors.

In a special ceremony Lawrence was awarded a rare honor — the Pierre de Coubertin Medal for sportsmanship. "By your sportsmanship, self-sacrifice, and courage, you embody all that is right with the Olympic ideal," the president of the International Olympic Committee told him.

When fighting broke out, Chuck Pelletier made the first of many decisions that changed the course of events that day.

FEAR IN ROOM 7

Everyone staying at Hotel Orchid in the Democratic Republic of the Congo was afraid that day. At first the fear was whisper-small and easy to control. The *rat-tat-tat* of machine-gun fire was far away; the boom of exploding grenades dull and distant. As the fighting moved closer to the hotel, as bullets tore through windows and mortar shells ripped holes in walls, fear grew. It crept through the lobby, down the hall into Room 7.

The Democratic Republic of the Congo, a country in Central Africa, has a long history of instability; violent outbreaks are common. With the first elections in four decades about to take place, tensions were higher than usual. To preserve peace — to make sure that democracy had a fair chance — the United Nations had sent a number of workers and volunteers to the Congo. One of them was Charles "Chuck" Pelletier, a thirty-eight-year-old Canadian peacekeeper with twenty years' experience in the military.

When fighting between rebels and border guards broke out on the evening of Wednesday, May 26, 2004, Chuck, who had friends staying at nearby Hotel Orchid, reacted swiftly. After ensuring that everyone connected to the UN was safe in a compound down the road, he drove his white pickup truck to the hotel.

"I went back to the hotel because my friends were there," he explained. "When something like that happens you get really close really fast. I wanted to make sure they were okay."

That night Chuck chose to stay with his friends at the hotel, outside the ring of protection that the UN compound would have provided him. At 5 A.M., gunfire woke him. An hour later bursts of rocket and mortar fire rocked the hotel. Grabbing his blue peacekeeper's helmet and a flak jacket, Chuck headed to the hotel lobby. About forty panic-stricken men and women were there, some standing alone, others huddled in groups, all of them scared, confused, and uncertain what to do.

The group needed a leader, and Chuck quickly took charge.

Even though he was a volunteer—a peacekeeper, not a soldier in this situation—Chuck had experience in combat zones. The group needed a leader, and Chuck quickly took charge. He herded the hotel guests down to the main floor and into Room 7. They would be safer here, he figured, crammed into a small room, protected by concrete, away from bullets spraying the windows of the upper floor, away from mortar fire landing just 130 feet away.

Some of the guests were diplomats and officials. Others were reporters, photographers, filmmakers, or visitors to the country. Included in the group were three members of Sum 41, a Canadian rock band who had been visiting refugee camps in the Congo for a documentary film. Most in Room 7 were strangers to each other, united by circumstances and a common emotion — fear.

The situation seemed hopeless. They were trapped and the fighting was getting closer. Chuck tried not to show fear to others in the room, but he could feel his morale fading. "I was pretty much absolutely sure that I was going to die at this point," he said later.

Speaking quietly so no one else could hear, Chuck phoned his wife, Christine, and left her a message. "If I don't make it home, I love you very much."

Figuring they might be in for a long stay and would need more space, Chuck divided the forty guests into three groups, leaving one group in Room 7 and assigning the others two rooms nearby. He gave strict instructions — stay quiet and don't move. Then he began to plot their escape.

First he radioed the UN compound for help. He was

Volunteer peacekeeper Chuck Pelletier.

told to flee, to come back to the base where it was safe. As tempting as it was, Chuck knew he couldn't leave. "No, I've got to stay here," he argued. "There's, like, forty people here that don't know what the hell they're doing and they need somebody to take care of them."

Chuck convinced the UN to send armored personnel carriers to the hotel. Bulletproof, built like small tanks, these armored vehicles could transport ten individuals at a time to the safety of the UN compound. With the promise of help on the way, Chuck numbered the guests and organized them into smaller groups. All

A UN armored personnel carrier in the Congo.

the while gunfire moved closer and shells rocked the building.

"As we were crouched outside getting our number," a member of Sum 41 said, "a mortar bomb exploded [30 feet] from our hotel which shook the entire hotel and blasted bricks off the roof."

That afternoon an armored personnel carrier finally appeared. Soldiers popped through the top of the carrier to provide cover. After giving strict orders to "walk, not run" down the dirt road, Chuck used his own body as a shield to escort the first group to the vehicle. When one group was safely on its way, he prepared the next for its turn.

One group at a time, the frightened guests were taken to the UN compound a mile away. Finally Chuck took his turn. Loading the last few guests in his pickup truck, he rushed them there himself.

Thanks to Chuck's actions, his steely calmness, and his determination in the face of fear, forty-two people were led to safety that day. In appreciation Sum 41 named the album they released later that year *Chuck* — for the man who rescued them. In 2007 Chuck Pelletier received national recognition for his heroism when he was awarded the Medal of Bravery by the governor-general of Canada.

> *"I wasn't the hero that day. I was just a guy with a little training and a little stupid."*
>
> — CHUCK PELLETIER

Caught between two worlds on the remote mountain, Simon Yates and Joe Simpson faced impossible choices.

TRUST IN EVERY STEP

For Joe Simpson and Simon Yates, the climb up the western face of Siula Grande in the Peruvian Andes had been

Climbing mountains requires a delicate balance of risk-taking and extreme caution.

painstakingly slow. A toehold here. A thin ledge there. A rope connecting the two men. Trust in every step.

The 20,800-feet mountain is notorious for its sharp spires, icy folds, deep fissures, and hidden dangers. But the two friends were up to the challenge. They had climbed together before and, as always, they exercised caution.

When they reached the top, Joe and Simon celebrated briefly, taking pictures and congratulating each other. Then, with darkness bearing down on them, they turned to practical matters — scooping out a snow cave, firing up the camp stove, and hunkering down for the cold night ahead.

The next morning, June 8, 1985, the two men broke camp and started the long climb down. It was 10 miles to their base camp and a storm was on its way. Joe, in the lead, used his ice ax to navigate the tricky slope. Simon followed. As a safety measure, a long rope connected the men.

Suddenly on a cliff 5,000 feet below the summit, the rope was put to the test. Joe fell and slid into a rock wall, smashing his right knee. Then he catapulted backward and careened down the mountain. He finally jerked to a stop, saved from falling farther by the safety rope. The pain in his leg was agonizing, and while Simon clambered down the slope to his aid, Joe fought to stay conscious.

A quick look at Joe's leg told the harsh truth. He was too badly injured to make it to base camp. Simon would be risking his own life if he tried to help Joe descend.

Even so, Simon tried. He hollowed out a seat in the snow to sit in. Holding one end of the rope firmly in his hands, the other end still fastened to Joe, Simon slowly paid out the rope, lowering Joe down the mountain slope inch by inch. To guide himself, Joe used his good leg, but each tug of the rope, every bump along the jagged rocks, brought a fresh stab of pain.

When the rope reached its end, Joe carved out a new seat in the snow while Simon climbed down. Then they repeated the slow process — Simon lowering Joe, Joe fighting the pain, rappelling down the mountain with his one good leg, then carving out a seat for Simon when the rope ran out.

For nine hours, as a storm lashed the mountain, the two men continued the slow descent. When they finally cleared the steepest section, they breathed easier. The worst was over, they thought.

Then disaster. Joe skidded on an icy patch. He swung the ice ax to anchor himself, but failed. Unable to stop, he slipped over the edge of a cliff. Again the rope held. Joe jerked to a halt and dangled in space, caught between two worlds. Far above him Simon still clutched the rope. Far below him was a gaping crevasse and a bottomless void.

Joe screamed in anguish, but the howling wind washed his voice away.

Simon held on. He dug in his heels, anchored his body, and gripped the rope tight. Joe was deadweight, impossible to pull up. All Simon could do was prevent Joe from falling farther. But was Joe even still alive? Unable to see below or hear Joe's voice, Simon had no way of knowing.

Death for one or both of them was inescapable.

Night was approaching and the storm was in full fury. The cold took its toll. Simon's fingers grew numb and stiff. He knew he couldn't hang on forever. Eventually he would tire, loosen his grip, and drop Joe. Either that or be dragged over the edge himself. Death for one or both of them was inescapable.

For an hour Simon held on, debating his choices. Finally he reached into his backpack and pulled out a knife.

For Joe, hanging off the cliff of a mountain, time seemed at a standstill. His leg ached horribly, and he wondered how Simon was doing. Then suddenly he felt the rope slacken, the pull of gravity, and his body falling. As he dropped, Joe's mind scrambled to make sense of it.

To his surprise the fall wasn't long, just 60 feet. He landed on a small ice ledge, his injuries no worse than before. Joe dug out his flashlight and studied his surroundings. He was in a huge cavern of ice encircled by walls too steep to climb. Below the ledge there was only unending blackness.

Joe reeled in the rope and checked the end. It was frayed, and that could mean only one thing. Simon had cut the rope, giving him up for dead. Now he was trapped in an icy tomb with no possibility of escape.

That night passed slowly for Joe, interrupted by tears and blackened by despair.

Morning brought fresh perspectives for both men.

After cutting the rope Simon had spent the night alone on the mountain. He had done everything humanly possible to help Joe, he told himself. But Joe was dead now and he had to think of himself. What other option did he have? He headed for base camp.

Meanwhile, with sunlight penetrating his tomb, Joe saw again that there was no way to climb the steep walls. If he stayed where he was, he would die eventually. One slim hope remained. Perhaps there was a way out farther down.

He had 150 feet of rope. With one end anchored to the ice with an ice screw, Joe threw the rest of the rope into the chasm. In spite of the pain he started to slither down the rope. When he reached the end he discovered that he was dangling just above a snow-covered floor. It veered upward toward a sunlit crack in the ice at the top.

Joe let himself drop. Keeping himself as flat as possible to spread out his weight, he crawled along the fragile shelf toward the patch of light above. Five hours later he reached the opening and wiggled through. Breathing in the fresh mountain air, he gazed at the valley far below. He was grateful to be alive, but now he faced an even greater challenge — reaching base camp.

Equipment such as ice screws and ice axes are essential climbing gear.

Simon would be there by now, Joe knew. So would Richard Hawking, a crew member who had stayed behind to tend their things. They would likely be preparing to leave, believing that he was dead. His only chance for survival was to get to the base camp before they departed.

Using the ice ax Joe pulled himself down the icy slope. When darkness fell, he spent the night in a snow hole. The next day he continued his journey. When the ice thinned, exposing rocks on the trail, he fashioned a makeshift splint by strapping foam from his sleeping bag around his leg and, using the ice ax as a walking stick, hobbled forward.

Joe set twenty-minute goals for himself and kept his mind occupied by reciting passages from Shakespeare. He was weak from lack of food and water, his fingers were frostbitten, and his mind played tricks with reality. He heard a voice in his head giving him directions as he wandered down the mountain.

Around 3 A.M. on June 12, four days after he'd fallen into the crevasse, a putrid smell greeted him. To Joe it was the most wonderful of smells. It came from the base camp latrines. He saw lights in the distance and heard voices that sounded familiar, but he was too weak to continue. Though he cried for help, his whimpers were barely audible.

Fortunately Simon and Richard Hawking heard his cry while they were packing up and getting set to leave. They searched for the source of the sound and found Joe — frail, sobbing, giggling, delirious with relief . . . and alive, though it didn't seemed possible.

News of Joe Simpson's miraculous escape from Siula Grande circled the globe, propelled in good part by a book he wrote about the ordeal called *Touching the Void*.

Today Joe Simpson and Simon Yates still climb mountains, though not together as they once did. They lead separate lives and remain cordial, not strong friends, but still respectful of each other. Mountains, they know, have a way of changing people, and since that extraordinary climb down Siula Grande, they have moved on, preferring to live in the present rather than dwell in the past.

> *"You saved my life you know. It must have been terrible for you that night. I don't blame you. You had no choice. I understand that, and I understand why you thought I was dead."*
>
> — JOE SIMPSON TO SIMON YATES, *TOUCHING THE VOID*

"All my agonizing after cutting the rope had not changed anything. My decision had been right; we had both survived. . . . I have met people who are understanding of my actions and others who are openly hostile. Their second-hand opinions mean nothing compared to the words Joe uttered to me in the tent that night in Peru."

— SIMON YATES, *AGAINST THE WALL*

En route to their cottage, eleven-year-old Leia Hunt-Hans and her father, David, caught one of their snowmobile skis on a snag. The snowmobile plunged down a steep ravine, crashed through an ice-covered creek, and pinned David, fracturing his knee in five places. After helping her father out of the ravine, Leia gathered firewood and started a fire to keep him warm. Then she walked for two hours to search for help.

Cold, terrified by howling wolves, and unable to locate anyone, she circled back in darkness and huddled beside her dad through the −17° Fahrenheit night. The following morning she tried again, this time walking 4 miles in ice-caked boots before encountering snowmobilers who told her that her father had been rescued.

Although she survived, Leia spent three months in the hospital, during which time her right foot and left toes had to be amputated due to the frostbite she had suffered.

In 2004 Leia Hunt-Hans was awarded the Star of Courage, an honor given only for extreme acts of bravery in circumstances of great peril.

Wesley Autrey saw the young man buckle and fall just as the headlights of the No. 1 train appeared. He had two options and only seconds to decide.

LEAP OF FAITH

The subway station at 137th Street and Broadway in New York City was busy as usual. It was just before 12:45 P.M., and people were milling around the platform. Most were strangers to each other. Many were in a rush.

Twenty-year-old Cameron Hollopeter, a New York Film Academy student, was there, just another face in the crowd, waiting along with everyone else. So was Wesley Autrey, a fifty-year-old construction worker. He was on the platform with his daughters Syshe and Shuqui, waiting for the train that would shuttle the girls home to their mother before Wesley headed off to his night-shift job.

Just before the No. 1 train was scheduled to arrive, Cameron had a seizure. Without warning, the nerve cells in part of his brain misfired, shooting impulses through his body that caused his muscles to spasm. He collapsed on the platform, arms thrashing and legs jerking uncontrollably.

Wesley saw Cameron go down and rushed to help. Two women joined him. While they tended to Cameron, Wesley raced across the station to call for help. By the time he returned, Cameron seemed better. The young man had staggered to his feet, but he was unsteady, weaving across the platform, teetering dangerously close to the edge. Then, in front of Wesley and dozens of other horrified witnesses, he toppled off, falling on the subway tracks just as the headlights of the No. 1 train appeared.

Time seemed to stand still for Wesley. He had a split second to make his decision: stand on the platform with

New Yorker Wesley Autrey stands on the subway platform at 137th and Broadway.

his young daughters at his side and watch disaster unfold, or risk his own life and do something to help the young man.

Leaving his daughters in the care of one of the women, Wesley jumped down onto the track. He grabbed Cameron, thinking he could haul him back up to the platform, but a quick glance over his shoulder told him that was impossible. The train was too close and the young man was struggling in confusion, not knowing who Wesley was or why he had pounced on him.

Wesley made another split-second decision. Grabbing Cameron in a bear hug, he pulled him away from the dangerous, high-voltage third rail and rolled toward the center of the tracks. There was a shallow drainage trough there, a grimy gutter 8 to 12 inches deep. Wesley pinned his hopes, and the lives of both of them, on it.

The train was too close and the young man was struggling in confusion.

Cameron landed in the gutter with Wesley on top. The young man squirmed, pushing against Wesley to throw him off.

"Don't move!" Wesley said. "Or one of us is going to lose a leg."

The train rumbled closer, brakes squealing in an

attempt to stop in time. The sound drowned out shouts and screams from the platform. One car thundered over them. Then a second. Wesley felt the rush of air on his neck. He pressed down harder, flattening himself as much as possible. The undercarriage was just inches above him, the wheels an arm's length away.

The train screeched to a stop with the two men, amazed to still be alive, underneath. For a moment there was silence, then Wesley heard the sound of crying from the platform. His daughters were still there. They'd seen the train roll over him.

"We're okay," he yelled. "I've got two daughters up there. Let 'em know their father's okay!"

Applause and cheers poured from the platform.

"Who are you?" asked Cameron.

"Someone who saved your life," Wesley told him.

It took approximately twenty minutes for technicians to cut the power to the third rail and extract the men from beneath the train. Cameron was rushed to a nearby hospital, cut and bruised, but otherwise unhurt. Wesley refused treatment, and after visiting Cameron in the hospital, continued with his day. He dropped his daughters off as planned and headed to work.

News of Wesley's act spread throughout the city. His boss bought him a ham-and-cheese hero sandwich and told him to take the rest of the day off. One city newspaper called him the "Subway Hero," another

Although the driver engaged the emergency brake, the subway train could not stop in time. Two cars thundered over the men on the track.

the "Subway Superman." Strangers stopped him on the street, shook his hand, and slapped him on the back to offer congratulations.

Other surprises followed—interviews on national talk shows, a $10,000 check from Donald Trump, free tickets to concerts and baseball games, scholarships and computers for his daughters, trips to Disney World for his family. On January 4, 2007, two days after the incident, New York mayor Michael Bloomberg presented Wesley with the Bronze Medallion, the city's highest award for exceptional citizenship.

"I don't feel like I did something spectacular; I just saw someone who needed help. I did what I felt was right."

— WESLEY AUTREY

CALLED TO ACTION | **December 8, 2003 / Toronto, Canada**

The first paramedic on the scene after a downtown Toronto building collapsed heard the cries for help coming from the debris. He found a ten-year-old boy, Seung Woo Cho, pinned under a beam. Under the rubble, he also saw the hair and shirt of a man — twenty-seven-year-old Augusto Cesar Mejia Solis. Augusto was dead, crushed under a collapsed wall. His body was partly covering the boy, who was injured, but very much alive thanks to Augusto's final act.

Investigators believe that as the wall crumbled, Augusto protected the boy from falling bricks and masonry by using his own body as a shield.

CALLED TO ACTION | **November 2, 2002 / California, U.S.A.**

When an ultralight plane flying above California's Redlands Municipal Airport lost its wheel, twelve-year-old Dustin Baker reacted quickly. Knowing that without the wheel the plane could crash upon landing, Dustin grabbed the wheel, jumped into an airport emergency vehicle, and tore down the runway. "I didn't stop to think I shouldn't be driving," he said later. The sixth grader's only driving experience had been around the desert near their home with his dad.

When the plane approached, Dustin pulled over, switched on the emergency light, jumped on the hood, and waved the wheel over his head. Alerted to the danger, the pilot was able to prepare for an emergency landing by slowing the plane and bringing it down safely, away from other aircraft. "I think it was very heroic," pilot Randy Lehfeldt said of Dustin's action. "He was a take-charge guy."

CHAPTER 3

AT THE EDGE OF INJUSTICE

It is our choices, Harry, that show
what we truly are, far more
than our abilities.

—J. K. ROWLING,

HARRY POTTER AND THE CHAMBER OF SECRETS

*When the Nazis herded the Jews of Warsaw
into a ghetto, Irena Sendlerowa could not stand
idly by.*

IRENA'S SECRET

In Warsaw, Poland, along an ordinary city street stands an ordinary apple tree. It is old and gnarled, and has stood in the same garden for decades. It was there in September 1939 when Poland was invaded by Nazi Germany, an event that marked the start of World War II. It was there, too, when Irena Sendlerowa, a twenty-nine-year-old social worker, fought in secret to save the lives of the Jews of Warsaw, targets of Nazi oppression. In fact, in a way, the apple tree—ordinary and unremarkable—was Irena's silent partner.

In the fall of 1940, after a year of stripping Jews of their bank accounts, homes, and possessions, the Nazis stepped up their operations. They rounded up Warsaw's Jews and herded them into a sixteen-block section of the city. Behind the 10-foot-high ghetto walls, four hundred and forty-five thousand Jews lived in cramped, crowded conditions. Food was scarce, infection spread, and the death toll climbed. Five thousand people died from starvation and disease each month. Worse yet, the Nazis made daily visits to select hundreds of people to cram into crowded boxcars bound for concentration camps.

Irena Sendlerowa, an administrator with the Warsaw Social Welfare Department, felt she could not stand idly by. As a child, she had seen her father, a doctor, help the poor and unfortunate, expecting little for himself in return. "I was brought up to believe that a person must be rescued when drowning, regardless of religion and nationality," she explained.

Irena joined Zegota, a secret resistance group dedicated to helping Jews. Disguised as a nurse, she

In the spring of 1943, an uprising in the ghetto was put down by German troops. In this photo, Jewish mothers and children are forcibly pulled out of hiding places and deported to concentration camps.

infiltrated the heavily guarded ghetto. Often she brought along a colleague or two, non-Jews like her. They visited families, administering medicine to avoid suspicion, but intent on something far riskier — smuggling Jews, especially children, out of the ghetto.

Convincing parents to give up their children to a stranger was difficult. Irena wore a Star of David armband to earn the parents' trust, but still the scene was an emotional one — children clinging to their mothers, pleading and crying; fathers clutching their children, not wanting to let them go, but knowing they must.

"Can you guarantee that we will see our children again?" the parents often asked.

"No, I cannot," Irena would answer. "But I can guarantee they will die if they stay."

Irena whisked the children away, cautioning them to be quiet, for the journey out of the ghetto was dangerous. The slightest noise might attract the attention of the Nazi guards and put all of their lives in jeopardy. Frequently their escape was by ambulance, Irena in the front seat, the children hidden in sacks, boxes, body bags, or coffins in the back. Sometimes Irena sedated the children, administering drugs to calm their nerves or lull them to sleep. Other times a small dog sat on the seat beside her, a yappy animal whose excited barks drowned any sounds the children made.

There were other ways out of the ghetto, and Irena used them, too. Sewers and secret underground passages.

Holes in the ghetto wall. A church with two exits, one leading into the ghetto, the other leading beyond its walls. Children who could mumble a few words of a Christian prayer could be quickly ushered past the guards who patrolled the exit out to the rest of the city.

Once outside the ghetto the children were given new names and false family histories. They were instructed to tell no one that they were Jews. A network of fellow conspirators helped place the children in homes, orphanages, and convents around the country.

"No one ever refused to take a child from me," Irena said.

As a last step in the process Irena made a trip to a neighbor's garden. There, under an apple tree, she buried glass jars stuffed with tissue paper. Written on each piece of paper was the original name and new identity of a child she had smuggled out of the Warsaw ghetto. It was Irena's hope that after the war these clues would help parents locate their children, or at the very least, give the children back their real names.

"No one ever refused to take a child from me," Irena said.

The risk for Irena if she was caught at any time during her secret operation was death. In occupied Poland it was not uncommon for people to simply disappear.

Citizens of Warsaw lived in fear that the Nazi police would come for them for the slightest of reasons.

For sixteen months Irena continued her dangerous mission, rescuing over twenty-five hundred children from the ghetto. Then on October 20, 1943, she was arrested by the Gestapo. Another member of Zegota had been caught and tortured until forced to tell Irena's name and address. Irena was interrogated for hours, and beaten. Her legs and arms were broken. But she refused to reveal the names of the children or the identities of the other rescuers.

"I was quiet as a mouse. I would have rather died than disclose anything about our operations," she said.

Irena was sentenced to death. On the day of her execution, a German guard who had been bribed by Zegota helped her escape. Irena's name was falsely posted on a list of those executed and, for a time, the Nazis believed she was dead. When they discovered the truth, they redoubled their efforts, anxious to bring her rescue attempts to an end.

For the remainder of the war, Irena went underground. To be captured again would jeopardize the entire operation. But despite being beaten, having put her friends and family in danger, and being forced into hiding, Irena continued her secret work. Instead of giving up on what she believed was right, she helped the cause where she could. Yet Irena—after the war and for the rest of her life—would be haunted by feelings that she hadn't done enough to save Warsaw's Jews.

When the war finally ended Irena recovered the glass jars from under the apple tree. With her lists of names, she spent years tracking down the children she had rescued, informing them of their true identities and reconnecting them when possible with relatives. Unfortunately most had no family members left. Their parents, grandparents, aunts, and uncles had been gassed or shot in the concentration camps.

As the decades passed, governments changed and borders shifted. Life in Poland returned to a normal pace. Irena's valiant deeds were forgotten or ignored, and Irena herself preferred it that way. Then in 1999 four American teenagers uncovered Irena's story while working on a school history project about the Holocaust, and tracked her down. By now she was almost ninety years old, frail and crippled from the torture she had endured during the war but still very much the energetic person she had always been. The teenagers wrote a short play about her called *Life in a Jar*. With her story now public, Irena received a number of awards and commendations, including a nomination for the Nobel Peace Prize in 2007.

Surprised by all the attention, Irena Sendlerowa became a reluctant celebrity, and so, too, did the apple tree. No longer ordinary and unremarkable, it now stood for something quite remarkable — a story of heroic

Sixty years after the end of World War II, ninety-five-year-old Irena Sendlerowa met with one of the American teenagers who helped make her story known.

proportions where a single person gave life to thousands more.

> *"When the war started, all of Poland was drowning in a sea of blood, but most of all it affected the Jewish nation. And within that nation it was the children that suffered most. That's why we needed to give our hearts to them."*
>
> — IRENA SENDLEROWA

CALLED TO ACTION | The 1850s / Southern states, U.S.A.

When Alexander Milton Ross heard of the Underground Railroad, a network of secret routes, meeting points, and safe houses that helped escaped slaves reach freedom, the Canadian doctor and naturalist knew he had to get involved.

To get word of the Underground Railroad to slaves, Alexander adopted a clever, but daring, plan. Under the guise of being an ornithologist — a person who studies birds — he crossed the border and visited plantations in the southern United States. At a plantation Alexander made a simple request of the owners: Would they mind if he studied the birds on their estate? With their permission, he freely roamed the property, noting birds for the owner's satisfaction, but actually doing something else — making contact with slaves.

In secret Alexander told them the location of "stations," people they could trust, and dangers they should avoid on the trip to freedom. He gave them supplies — food, money, a knife or compass. On some occasions he accompanied groups of slaves, "conducting" them to safety in Canada himself.

Slave owners often posted want ads for the return of their missing slaves, sometimes offering rewards. Runaways who were caught risked beatings and even death for themselves and their

| **CALLED TO ACTION** | **The 1850s / Southern states, U.S.A.** |

families. The punishments for conductors and others caught helping slaves escape were swift and severe as well.

Alexander made several trips to the southern states, assisting in the antislavery cause, and successfully dodging detection. His birdwatching interests, it seems, were genuine. Later in life he published a number of books on nature and collected and classified hundreds of species of birds and other wildlife.

The two boys had been handpicked for death by Josef Mengele, Hitler's notorious henchman. It would take a bold step to save their lives.

TO THE LEFT, DEATH

At Birkenau Death Camp, fourteen-year-old Hellmuth Szprycer and thirteen-year-old Harry Lowit stood beside each other, naked and shivering, fearing the worst and hoping for the best, while waiting for the Angel of Death to decide. Would they live or would they die?

The two boys were not alone. Thousands of other prisoners huddled around them. Herded together like cattle, stripped of clothes and dignity, some were silent while others wept as they waited to hear their fate. At Auschwitz-Birkenau, the Nazi concentration camp in Brezezinka, Poland, life was a fragile thing, especially when Josef Mengele, the Angel of Death, paid a visit.

Birkenau was the cornerstone of the Nazi plan to exterminate Jews during World War II. There were other Nazi concentration camps across Europe, other places where prisoners were brought, but not one was designed for death in quite the same way as

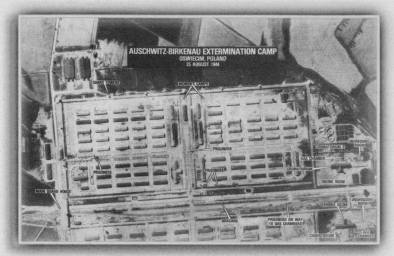

An aerial image of the Auschwitz-Birkenau camp taken by the U.S. Army Air Force in 1944. The rectangular buildings housed prisoners. The gas chambers are at the right.

Birkenau. At its peak, with its four giant gas chambers operational, its furnaces and ovens roaring, its towering chimneys spewing black smoke, up to ten thousand victims could be murdered in a single day, their bodies reduced to ash. During the three years that Birkenau functioned as a death camp, at least 1.1 million Jews and almost two hundred thousand other political prisoners lost their lives there.

One of the most feared Nazi officers at Birkenau was a slightly built, bland-looking man with a baby-doll face named Josef Mengele. As the chief doctor, Mengele frequently used prisoners, especially children, in hideous and cruel experiments. It was Mengele who decided who lived and who died. To the camp's inmates, he was known as the Angel of Death.

Periodically Mengele visited the camp to screen prisoners, handpicking some to use as human test subjects in the name of medical research, and deciding among the others who would be sent to the gas chambers. Those deemed healthy and useful were sent to a line on the right to work as slave laborers for the Nazis. Inmates judged useless — too old, too young, sick, weak, or unskilled — were sent to a line on the left. To the left meant death in the gas chambers.

That day in July 1944, Hellmuth and Harry were among the thousands forced to gather for inspection. The war had cost both boys everything — their families, homes, and belongings were all gone. Hellmuth and Harry had met for the first time at the camp. Since finding each other at Birkenau, they had stuck close together, doing whatever it took to stay alive, even if it meant cleaning boots for Nazi officers or running errands for them around the camp. Staying alive, the boys knew, meant keeping busy, looking productive, and giving the Nazis a reason for wanting to keep them around.

Hellmuth and Harry watched the Angel of Death stride through the crowd. He wore a small smile on his face as he pointed to a man here, a child there, directing people into lines left and right. Death to the left; life to the right.

After all, what did he have to lose? He'd already been condemned to death.

Mengele's steely eyes settled on Hellmuth, then on Harry. He wasted no time in deciding their fate. To the left, he ordered.

Hellmuth was quick to react. After all, what did he have to lose? He'd already been condemned to death. Taking a bold step forward, he approached the notorious Nazi doctor. "I want to work for you," Hellmuth said in German, looking straight into the Nazi's eyes. "I will do anything—clean your shoes, your motorcycle. Don't put me in the gas chamber."

Mengele stared at Hellmuth. "Where are you from?"

"Berlin," he answered.

Somehow the answer pleased Mengele. To Hellmuth's surprise, Mengele agreed to spare his life, and assigned him to serve as a messenger at the main gate.

Relieved, Hellmuth turned and started toward the line on the right. He would live now. But as he passed he saw Harry, wide eyed, silently pleading with him to speak on his behalf. Harry was from Prague,

Sentenced to death, these women and children walk toward the gas chambers.

Czechoslovakia—he didn't speak German. He couldn't barter with Mengele for his life.

For the second time Hellmuth approached the Angel of Death. As Harry huddled nearby, Hellmuth begged for his friend's life. It was a daring move. Mengele had just granted Hellmuth his own life. He could just as easily take it away.

Mengele eyed the boys, then, in a sick game of fate, he pulled out two matches, one shorter than the other. "The one who takes the longest match will live," he said. "The shortest goes to the gas chamber."

The boys pulled the matches. Harry got the short one.

It was decided. Hellmuth would live. Harry would die.

At the news Harry burst into tears. "I don't want to die," he cried.

For a third time, Hellmuth went to Mengele. "What's one more?" he boldly asked. He was playing a high-stakes game. What if Mengele became angry with him for begging for more?

Perhaps it was the boy's gutsy style, or the fact that he was from Germany. Maybe it was his determination to stay alive, or his willingness to stand up for his friend no matter the cost. But whatever the reason, Mengele agreed to Hellmuth's request. Both boys were assigned to be messengers. Hellmuth saved not only himself from the gas chamber that day, but his friend, too.

For the next few months the Nazis doubled their efforts to exterminate Europe's Jews. Record numbers of prisoners were sent to the gas chambers. Hellmuth and Harry kept busy working at the camp, dodging both death and Mengele's changeable ways.

In the winter of 1944–45, as Allied forces advanced closer to Birkenau, the remaining prisoners were force-marched back to Germany. Hellmuth and Harry became separated and, for almost fifty years, they lost touch.

Then, unknown to each other, they both agreed to be interviewed for a special Holocaust project overseen by filmmaker Steven Spielberg. A staff member noticed the similarities of their stories and put them in touch with one another.

The two men, once close as brothers and survivors of the Holocaust, were reunited in London, England, in 1997. They celebrated with food and drink, tears and laughter.

> *"Something in me gave me power.*
> *Death was on [one] side, but we got*
> *away with it."*
>
> — HELLMUTH SZPRYCER

*As tanks rumbled down the streets of Beijing,
one man stepped forward to meet them.*

HE STOOD ALONE

No one knows his name, where he came from, or where he went later. He appeared on a street in Beijing, China, on June 5, 1989 — an ordinary man dressed in slacks and a white shirt, a shopping bag in each hand. For a few moments, while the world watched and held its breath, he stood, simply stood.

It was a quiet act, born of desperation, yet so remarkable that today, decades later, it continues to live in video clips played daily on the Internet. For lack of a real name, the man has been dubbed Tank Man. Others call him the Unknown Rebel. Both names hint at the boldness of his act and the reasons we remember it today.

Beijing, the capital of the People's Republic of China, is a bustling, modern city. At its center, flanked by majestic buildings, ornamental gates, and wide boulevards, lies Tiananmen Square. It is the world's largest outdoor plaza, a space so big that a million people could fit in the open courtyard.

In 1989 a series of events brought citizens of Beijing to Tiananmen Square. It started on April 17, when ten thousand university students gathered there to mourn the death of a widely-respected political leader who had promoted reform. The Chinese Communist Party, which ruled the country, was criticized for controlling the press, the economy, and people's actions too tightly. The students called out for greater freedom and sweeping political change.

Each day the number of students in Tiananmen Square grew. Soon they were joined by thousands of teachers, doctors, and industrial workers. Together the protestors

Demonstrating students surround policemen near Tiananmen Square. In the early days of the protest, authorities were so outnumbered by demonstrators that they were powerless to control the crowd.

held hunger strikes, waved placards, and staged sit-ins in a quest to obtain democratic rights for the people of China.

For a while China's rulers tolerated the protest, hoping that in time it would settle itself. But as weeks passed and the number in Tiananmen Square swelled to a million, traffic snarled, universities closed, and factories shut their doors. Word of China's unrest spread around the globe.

On May 19 the government declared martial law, and the military was given control of the city. The next day troops marched into Beijing with orders to clear the Square using peaceful measures. Hearing of the plan, protesters blocked convoys of tanks and trucks, started conversations with soldiers, and even provided them with food and water. Surrounded, unable to advance to Tiananmen Square or to withdraw from the city, the troops were stranded and at the mercy of the growing crowd.

For three days the standoff continued until protesters allowed the troops to leave on May 24. While the crowd celebrated their victory in Tiananmen Square, the government plotted its next move, determined more than ever to crush the pro-democracy movement.

Troops marched toward Tiananmen Square, leaving dead and wounded in their wake.

It came on June 3 when hundreds of thousands of troops stormed into the city from all corners. This time China's government troops were heavily equipped with tanks and artillery. Protesters flooded the streets bent on stopping these soldiers as they had the others. These soldiers, however, weren't interested in their food or conversation. As ordered, they opened fire with AK-47s, catching the unarmed civilians totally by surprise.

In the hours that followed, gunfire filled the air. Troops marched toward Tiananmen Square, leaving dead and wounded in their wake, and arresting those who stood in their way. Recognizing the futility of their struggle, the protesters scattered.

In a show of might, tanks and trucks rattled down the streets leading to Tiananmen Square. On Chang'an Boulevard, a major corridor leading to Tiananmen Square, onlookers watched from the safety of sidewalks and upper-story windows, too frightened to make a move. No one dared stand in the way now. The struggle for democracy seemed to be over.

Then a man appeared, calmly walking down the middle of the street. He was dressed in slacks and a white shirt, and carried a shopping bag in each hand. The column of tanks rumbled toward him, but instead of moving aside, the man continued walking in their direction. When the lead tank was just a few yards away, the man stopped and stood in the middle of the street. The tank edged closer. The man remained standing. Just when it seemed the tank would squash him, it stopped. The tanks behind were forced to halt as well.

For a few seconds the man stared at the tank. Then the tank swung left, as if to go around. The man shuffled a few steps, too, putting himself directly in line. The tank swerved to the right. The man moved again, planting himself in front of the tank once more. There was stunned silence from the crowd. People seemed to be holding their breath, waiting, wondering. What was the man doing, risking his life in this way, the day after a bloody massacre?

In a brazen act, "Tank Man," a defenseless protester, stared down a mighty tank and the government it stood for.

The tank stopped, engine idling. Finally, perhaps impatient with the game, the man dropped his bags, scrambled up on top of the tank to the hatch and pounded on it with his hand. The hatch opened. A head appeared. The man said a few words to the operator, then scrambled off and resumed his position in front of the tank.

Moments later two people appeared and pulled the man aside. He melted into the crowd, as anonymous as at the start. In minutes the encounter was over.

Tank Man's actions were captured on video, and within hours broadcast on televisions around the world. Audiences watched, transfixed at the image of a single person taking such a bold step. The act symbolized the pro-democracy movement where, for a short time, the citizens of Beijing stood their ground, peacefully demanding change, staring down a government more powerful than themselves.

CALLED TO ACTION　**October 31, 2004 / Ukraine**

The race for the leadership of Ukraine was close, and the stakes were high. Two main candidates were in the running. One was the sitting prime minister, Viktor Yanukovych, who had the support of Russia, Eastern Europe's largest and most powerful country. The opposing candidate was Viktor Yushchenko, leader of the Our Ukraine party.

On October 31 the election results were in. Yanukovych collected 39.32 percent of the vote; Yushchenko 39.87 percent. According to Ukrainian law, if no candidate had a clear 50 percent majority, a second election had to be held between the two leading finalists. The Yanukovych government, though, ignored the law and refused to hold a run-off election. There were complaints of corruption, fraud, and voter intimidation against Yanukovych and his supporters. The validity of the entire first vote was in question.

Yushchenko's party called on the public to protest the violation, and Ukrainians took to the streets. Rallies and marches took place, some involving a million people, many wearing orange ribbons or carrying orange flags, the color of the Our Ukraine party.

Known as the Orange Revolution, the protest proved effective. Together the citizens of Ukraine pressured for change. Swayed by the show of people, the Supreme Court ordered a revote for December 26. This time it was a clear majority for Yushchenko, who was later sworn in as president. The victory, though, was more than just Yushchenko's. It also belonged to the people of Ukraine.

With his village destroyed, his family shot or scattered, ten-year-old Michael Mayen began a 1,000-mile journey.

JOURNEY OF A LOST BOY

The day the soldiers came with their machine guns, Michael Mayen was in the fields outside his village doing what was expected of Sudanese boys his age—herding cattle, making sure the animals were safe and well fed.

It was 1987 and Sudan was embroiled in a bloody civil war—northern Sudan against southern Sudan, Arab against non-Arab, government forces against rebels. Attacks on villages in southern Sudan were common. Heavily armed soldiers arrived in convoys, supposedly to capture rebels. But the soldiers were more interested in killing men, and forcing women and children into slavery. Raided villages were burned afterward to squelch any future possibility of trouble from the region.

From the fields Michael heard bursts of artillery fire, the thunder of bombs exploding, and screams of terror. He saw smoke spiraling into the sky, and villagers scurrying for cover with soldiers in pursuit. With other boys,

Michael ran into some thick bushes to hide. When the soldiers fired into the bushes, the boys scrambled, found new hiding places, and waited until soldiers gave up the search.

There was nothing to stay for—only the possibility of death or capture.

When the smoke had cleared and the soldiers had left, Michael and the other boys came out from hiding. Their village had been destroyed and their families shot, captured, or scattered. They were suddenly all alone in the world, in a dangerous country with soldiers and rebels constantly on the prowl. What should they do? Running away seemed like the only option. There was nothing to stay for—only the possibility of death or capture. But where should they go? Where would it be safe?

Some thought they should head to Ethiopia, a country to the east. Others said no, that Kenya or Uganda, countries to the south, would be better. After some discussion, Ethiopia was chosen. The boys, ranging in age from five to thirteen, set out, most with nothing more than the clothes they had on. They would travel by foot to Ethiopia, hundreds of miles away. It would take many weeks.

They left their cattle behind. The animals required food and water, commodities difficult to find in Sudan's drought-stricken climate. Besides, cattle would attract soldiers, making the boys targets on the open road.

As they walked they met other boys with similar stories, on similar journeys. Their villages had also been destroyed, their families lost and scattered.

One group joined another and their numbers gradually swelled. "That," says Michael, "is where the gathering started." Small boys, tall boys, toddlers and teenagers, hundreds then thousands — a long river of humanity, all marching to Ethiopia.

Like most of the others, Michael carried nothing. Barefoot, he had no food or water, no protection from rain or cold, disease or wild animals. He scrounged the countryside for food as he traveled, plucking wild fruit off trees, sampling tall grasses, avoiding plants he knew were poisonous.

On lucky days, he might stumble across a dead animal. The flesh provided badly needed protein. On the most desperate days he had no other choice but to drink his own urine.

Walking took its toll. Boys grew thin and frail. The weakest became easy prey for lions and other predators. Without proper nourishment or clean drinking water, the boys were prone to diseases like malaria and typhoid fever. Some dropped in heaps on the road, too ill or tired or discouraged to continue. When a boy died, his body was left where it fell. The others didn't have the energy or the time to dig a grave, or to give a proper burial.

Michael was one of twenty-five thousand boys who fled Sudan.

One day Michael cut his foot on a piece of wood. The wound bled and then became infected. Walking was slow and very painful. Ethiopia was still a long way off, and there was no point in turning around. He had no home to go back to. His village was gone, his family dead or missing. Michael began to lose hope. *How am I going to make it, hurt like this? We are going nowhere. Why should I even try?* he asked himself.

Then the other boys gathered around Michael. "Just a bit farther . . . just one day more," they coaxed him.

It worked. With encouragement from his friends, Michael found it in himself to keep going.

It took four months to reach Ethiopia and the refu-gee camp at the border town of Pinyudo. Michael lived in a tent there for four years. Without country or identity he was one of the "Lost Boys of Sudan," the name given to the almost twenty-five thousand boys who, like himself, had fled their war-ravaged homeland.

Then in 1991 an uprising in Ethiopia forced them to run again. The country was in turmoil. Food and supplies were scarce, and the new government wanted to rid itself of refugees. With the others, Michael decided to flee over the border, cross back into Sudan and then move south to Kenya, a country with a long history of stability.

Michael and the others waited until midnight to make their break. Under the cover of darkness, they hid from soldiers and ran along the riverbank, looking for a spot to cross the river. Ethiopian troops opened fire, killing some, wounding others. Michael dodged artillery fire and hid among bodies, pretending to be dead. It was impossible to see clearly, to tell enemy from friend. In Dinka, his native language, Michael whispered to those he met, "Are you one of us?" An answer given in Dinka assured him that the stranger was.

For many, crossing the Gilo River on the Ethiopia-Sudan border was the worst part. Michael did not know how to swim, and the prospect of entering the river was terrifying. Fortunately one of the boys had a rope, and two others were able swimmers. They ferried the rope to the other side and anchored it. Michael used the rope to haul himself over to safety. Other boys were not so fortunate. Hundreds drowned or were shot, others were eaten by crocodiles in the river.

Michael finally reached Kenya after weeks of walking across Sudan — past burned-out villages and over minefields. He had walked over 1,000 miles and had faced death by starvation, disease, gunfire, and drowning. He was thin, frail, and weak from the journey, but his spirit was unbroken.

In 1998 Michael arrived in Canada as a refugee. Eleven years after being forced to flee his village, he was safe at last.

> *"Growing up, I listened to stories villagers told about Sudan's past and how people survived troubles. I drew courage from those stories and from them learned how a person should act."*
>
> — MICHAEL MAYEN

For sixteen-year-old Marina Nemat, life in prison was no life at all, but the alternatives were even worse.

BARGAINING FOR LIFE

In January 1982, on the night of her scheduled execution, sixteen-year-old Marina Nemat stood in line with four other prisoners — two girls, two young men — her hands bound, her feet in rubber slippers. The cold wind swirled snowflakes through the air, but even through the haze Marina could see the wooden poles sticking out of the frozen ground about 20 feet ahead. This is where she and the others would die, tied to the poles and cut down by bullets from a firing squad.

Marina had been condemned to death at a trial held earlier. The trial had been kept secret, and Marina hadn't even *known* about it. She hadn't heard the exact charges against her, nor had she been given a chance to defend herself. In the Islamic Republic of Iran, under the dictatorship of Ayatollah Khomeini, basic human rights were largely ignored.

There were long lists of possible wrongdoings in

Iran — and the list seemed to be longer for women than men. Simply being accused of an infraction or even suspected of one was enough to get arrested. Women had to cover themselves with long robes and scarves or wear the *chador*, a traditional flowing garment. Perfume, makeup, lipstick, nail polish — these were strictly forbidden. So, too, were participating in rallies or demonstrations, belonging to an "illegal" political party, and criticizing Islam or the government of Ayatollah Khomeini.

It was Marina's decision to speak out against the Islamic government that had gotten her into trouble. At school one day when her math teacher praised the government in what seemed to Marina like endless propaganda, she grew tired of listening. "I don't mean to be rude, Miss," Marina said, "but can we please get back to our main subject?"

"If you don't like what I'm teaching, you can leave the classroom," the teacher answered.

So Marina did. She gathered her books and left the room. But she was also followed by most of her classmates, which precipitated a student strike that lasted for three days. Her name was put on the principal's list of rebellious students. She was acting against the Islamic government, a crime punishable by death. The strike ended, but later Marina and some friends wrote articles about their political views in a school newspaper. That, too, got her into trouble.

At nine o'clock on the night of January 15, 1982, two armed revolutionary guards arrested Marina at her home. She was whisked away to Evin prison on the outskirts of Tehran, the capital city. To force her to release the names of other students, she was severely beaten on the soles of her feet with a cable.

"I don't know anything," Marina told her torturer.

But Marina did know. She knew the names of the students who had stormed out of class and those who had written articles. To confess their names would put them and their families in danger. They could be arrested, put in prison for months, possibly years, subjected to torture, even sentenced to death. And so Marina kept quiet, enduring each blow until the beating ended.

Marina had failed the test. To the government, she was a traitor.

Later, after it was over, Marina was told by one of the guards that they already had the names. The principal had provided them with the list. All they wanted was proof of her cooperation, her willingness to work with the government, not against it. Marina had failed the test. To the government, she was a traitor.

A trial was held in secret. Marina was condemned to death, and a few short hours later, she found herself with four others, facing the firing squad. The execution order was given, guns aimed, but before they could go off, a black car pulled up and stopped in front of the guards. A bearded man stepped out. He was holding a piece of paper — an official letter reducing Marina's death sentence to life in prison. Marina was untied. As she was being shuttled away the guns fired, ending the lives of the others.

The man who rescued her was named Ali. He was one of the guards who had arrested her earlier. He had also been present in the room when she was tortured. Somehow he had grown infatuated with her, and had gone directly to Ayatollah Khomeini, a close friend of his father's, to have Marina's death sentence changed to life in prison.

But in Marina's eyes, this was worse than death. It was life without freedom, family, or friends, in conditions that were deplorable, surrounded by other political prisoners, many facing death or torture.

"I didn't want anyone to save me. I wanted to die," Marina later wrote.

Marina now felt indebted to Ali, but he was a man she didn't trust, a man who stood for everything she hated about the Islamic government. There were strings attached to his act, she was sure, some motives that were unclear. The answer came a few months later when Ali came to visit her in prison and, to her astonishment, asked her to marry him.

Marriage would get Marina out of prison — Ali would see to that. He would give her a life again, a home, a new family. But she didn't love or trust Ali. Marriage to the man who had arrested her, who had watched while she was tortured, was unthinkable. "I can't marry you," she told Ali, flatly refusing him.

He was prepared for such an answer, and threatened to have her parents arrested and Andre, a man she secretly loved, tortured or even executed. What choice did Marina have? "I had put Andre and my parents in danger, and I had to do everything I could to protect them," she said.

So she agreed to Ali's proposal. And, forced by her husband, she converted from Christianity to Islam and moved into the house he had bought for them. Marriage was like a new prison for her. She was restricted by rules and obligations, unable to think and speak freely, or even to worship as she pleased. Yet to go against Ali risked putting Andre and her parents in danger.

Barely a week after the wedding, Ali received death threats from opponents of the Khomeini government. To protect his young wife, Marina was put back in prison. A few days later Ali was assassinated, and Marina found herself back where she had started. But this time she knew that she had done everything she could to protect those she loved from the consequences of her words and actions.

Eventually Marina was released from prison—two years, two months, and twelve days after her arrest. In time she married Andre and they left Iran to forge a new life together in Canada—a place without so many restrictions, where every act was not regarded with suspicion, and there was no torture, no death sentences.

Marina Nemat with her husband, Andre, in their home in Canada.

CALLED TO ACTION | **November 8, 1946 / Nova Scotia, Canada**

After buying a ticket to see a show in a New Glasgow movie theater, Viola Desmond took a seat on the ground floor. At the time many communities across Canada believed in segregation, where people were kept separate in public places based on the color of their skin. Viola was told that she was sitting in the "whites-only" section and that she would have to move to the "blacks-only" balcony level.

Viola went back to the ticket booth and demanded the more expensive ground-floor ticket. That was where she wanted to sit, not the balcony. When they refused to sell her the ticket, Viola went and sat on the ground floor anyway. The theater manager ordered her to move, but Viola refused. A policeman was called, and Viola was picked up out of her seat and carried into the street. There she was arrested and taken to jail for the night.

At a later trial, she was convicted on a charge of "tax evasion." She hadn't paid for the higher priced ground-floor seat, and the increased ticket price would have meant that the tax on the ticket was one penny more than she had paid. During the court case, the theater's segregated seating policy and the color of her skin were never mentioned.

Although Viola lost her court case, it raised discussions about segregation policies for the people of Nova Scotia. Thanks to Viola's courage, and others like her who stood up for social justice, people began to fight for equality and an end to racial segregation in the province.

In a country gone mad, quiet conversation and clever negotiation were Paul Rusesabagina's only weapons.

WHY RWANDA?

In Paul Rusesabagina's worst nightmares, he is back in Rwanda, the African country where he was raised, reliving the horrors of 1994 and asking himself, *Why?* Why did the country unravel as it did? Why did the rest of the world stand by and let it happen?

In 1994, 85 percent of Rwanda's six million people were Hutu; 15 percent Tutsi. The two ethnic groups spoke the same language, shared the same culture, married one another, and often lived side by side in the same neighborhoods. But native Rwandans knew one from the other, and for many, whether you were Hutu or Tutsi made all the difference in the world.

Like many African countries, Rwanda had once been a European colony, and during the colonial period, Tutsis and Hutus were treated differently. Believing the Tutsi to be more intelligent and "attractive," Europeans promoted many Tutsi to positions of power and privilege. The Hutu majority, meanwhile, were largely snubbed and treated as lower-class citizens.

For decades the unfair practice continued, creating deep divisions among the Rwandan people. In the late 1950s the Hutu majority took control, overthrowing the Tutsi monarchy in a bloody civil war that saw thousands of Tutsi massacred. By the time Rwanda achieved independence in 1962, hatred and resentment were deeply rooted, simmering just below the surface.

Violent outbreaks were still a common occurrence when, on the evening of Wednesday, April 6, 1994, a missile shot down a private jet carrying the Hutu president of Rwanda. Immediately the Tutsi were blamed for the attack. A Hutu civilian army, known as the Interahamwe, roamed the streets plucking Tutsi—referred to as "cockroaches"—from their homes. Anyone with a Tutsi connection became a target. Tutsis were shot on the spot or hacked to death with machetes.

That same evening, thirty-nine-year-old hotel manager Paul Rusesabagina was eating dinner on the terrace of the Diplomates Hotel in Kigali, the capital of Rwanda. Paul was skilled at his job—calm, fair, efficient, and, in his own words, "good at talking to people."

When word of the bombing reached Paul, he immediately rushed home. Although he was Hutu, his wife was Tutsi, and that meant his whole family was in danger.

That night, and for the next two days, the Rusesabaginas and their four children hid in the house, huddled around a radio to catch the latest news. Neighbors joined them. Relatives, too. By the morning of Saturday, April 9, thirty-one people were hiding in the Rusesabagina home, most of them Tutsi, all of them trusting Paul with their lives.

That same morning, two army jeeps filled with Interahamwe tore into the front yard. "We need you to open up the Diplomates," the captain demanded.

"I'd be happy to come, but I will need to take my family, too," Paul answered. Reluctantly, the captain agreed. Paul loaded his relatives and neighbors into two vehicles and, escorted by Interahamwe jeeps, they drove through deserted streets stained with blood and lined with bodies.

The caravan stopped and the captain got out and sauntered over to them. He held a rifle out to Paul. Paul got the captain's unspoken message loud and clear: We only need *you* to open the Diplomates. Prove your loyalty. Kill the others.

Forcing himself to be calm, Paul did what he did best—talk. In this situation, carefully chosen words were his only defense. He talked in terms the captain could understand. He told him there was money in the hotel safe. Lots of it. Paul would give it to the Interahamwe if everyone in his charge arrived there unharmed.

The bribe worked. The captain agreed to the conditions, and when they got to the hotel, Paul gave him the money as promised. Paul had just bought his family's lives. But what if the Interahamwe returned? How would Paul continue to keep them safe?

"Prove your loyalty. Kill the others."

A few days later Paul transferred his family to the Hotel des Mille Collines, another hotel in Kigali. He had once been assistant manager of the Mille Collines and he knew that the five-story luxury hotel would be safer, farther from mortar shells, looters, and rebels with itchy trigger fingers. Already hundreds of refugees were there, with more arriving each hour.

The hotel was an island of sanity in a country gone mad. At peak capacity the hotel could accommodate three hundred guests, but in no time there were over a thousand people at the Mille Collines.

Paul took responsibility for the "guests." After securing his family in one of the rooms, he went to the manager's office with his black leather binder. It contained the names and phone numbers of all the influential international contacts he had made over the years — army officers, ministers, doctors, professors — anyone who might return a favor in a time of need. Working through the binder, Paul placed call after call, begging for protection, asking for supplies, bargaining like never before. But little help came.

Meanwhile more people were arriving at the hotel. Paul managed to squeeze them into spaces that were already overflowing. No one was charged for rooms. "To take cash away from anyone would also be to strip them of money they might need to bribe their way out of being murdered," he said later.

Early on, power was cut to the hotel. Without lights or air conditioning, people lived in sweltering darkness. Before long they ran out of food and water, forcing Paul to be creative. He scoured hotel kitchens, raided lockers, smuggled goods into the hotel, and ordered staff to cook meals over fires built on the hotel lawn. He set up a ration system, treating everyone the same. Two meals a day. Two scoops of water from the hotel swimming pool. Small, equal portions for everybody.

As conditions worsened, Paul made more phone calls and sent faxes to foreign governments and the UN pleading for help. Most didn't seem to care. We have our own problems, was the basic response. Let Rwanda take care of its own.

To the Interahamwe, the Hotel Mille Collines was a thorn in its side. An average of five people a minute were dying in Rwanda — eight hundred thousand slaughtered within weeks. There, in that hotel, hundreds of Tutsis were hiding, evading Hutu justice. More than once, gun-toting Interahamwe arrived, spitting fury. Paul met each threat using quiet conversation and clever negotiation to defuse the situation.

One day an Interahamwe colonel arrived at the hotel. A death order had been issued against a journalist hiding there, and the colonel had come to execute the man.

"I've come to pick up that dog," the colonel told Paul.

Just 20 miles from the hotel, ten thousand Tutsis who had gathered in and around a Catholic church for protection were murdered by the Interahamwe. This victim was killed by a machete blow to the head.

Paul led the colonel to his office, sat him down, and offered him a drink. On the surface Paul seemed calm and in control. Inside he was nervous, his mind racing through a list of options. His only hope of saving the journalist was to keep the colonel talking, to use words to change his mind or divert his attention from his purpose.

Paul tried a number of approaches. First flattery. "You're too important a man for this kind of work," he told the colonel.

Next he tried guilt. Could the colonel live with the blood of this man on his hands, for his entire life? For more than two hours Paul switched topics and approaches, searching for a way to save the journalist. Nothing seemed to help.

Finally Paul changed his pitch. "I have some good red wine in the cellar. Let me bring you a carton. . . . Go home tonight and have a drink and we will talk more about this tomorrow. . . ." The colonel accepted the bribe, left, and never returned, the execution order against the journalist seemingly forgotten. Paul was relieved. He had put his own life on the line yet again.

Finally on May 26, with 1,268 people hiding in the hotel, the UN arrived to evacuate the refugees. After ensuring that everyone who wanted to leave was safely aboard, Paul hopped into the last jeep. As the long line of vehicles inched through the city, he hid under a black tarp. He was a marked man now — a Hutu who had protected Tutsis through a wave of bloodshed.

Eventually Paul and his family escaped to Tanzania. The rest of the world slowly woke up to the tragedy happening in Rwanda, and help from other countries began arriving. Paul moved to Belgium to start a new life. A book he wrote about his experience was the basis for the movie *Hotel Rwanda*.

Rwanda is still with Paul Rusesabagina today. It always will be. Nightmares are frequent visitors and so, too, are questions that trouble him. Why, he wonders, did it happen? Why did the world ignore Rwanda? Could it happen again?

> *"Words can be instruments of evil,*
> *but they can also be powerful tools of*
> *life. If you say the right ones they can*
> *save the whole world."*
>
> — PAUL RUSESABAGINA,
> *AN ORDINARY MAN*

CALLED TO ACTION | **1996 / Kabul, Afghanistan**

When the Taliban seized control of Afghanistan in 1996, they imposed rules on what could or could not be displayed in art. Depicting animals or humans in paintings or sculpture was strictly forbidden. Methodically the Taliban began destroying artwork they found offensive. Fearing that much of Afghanistan's culture would be lost forever, Muhammad Yousef Asefi, a physician and artist, came up with a dangerous plan to save over one hundred oil paintings for future generations. At the risk of being jailed or executed, he secretly began dabbing watercolor over the living creatures shown in the paintings, disguising the forbidden objects and replacing them with acceptable ones.

In 2001, when the Taliban government was finally pushed from power, Muhammad reversed the process. Using a wet sponge, he removed the watercolor, restoring the doctored paintings to their original condition. One man who dared to defy the Taliban saved centuries of art for the future generations of Afghanistan to enjoy.

CHAPTER 4

AT THE EDGE OF
THE IMPOSSIBLE

*Never doubt that a small group of
thoughtful, committed citizens can
change the world. Indeed, it is
the only thing that ever has.*

— MARGARET MEAD,

AMERICAN ANTHROPOLOGIST

Their plan was a wild one, and the chance of failure was greater than any chance of success.

LYNMOUTH'S CHALLENGE

On January 12, 1899, wind battered the tiny seaside village of Lynmouth, England, shattering windows and blasting doors. The fierce gale brought sheets of rain and tossed waves from the nearby Bristol Channel into the streets. Only the foolish dared venture outdoors.

That evening a telegram arrived, an urgent call for help from a nearby harbor town: VESSEL IN DISTRESS . . . CAN LYNMOUTH HELP?

The vessel in trouble was a large, three-masted sailing ship called the *Forrest Hall*. A tugboat had been towing it through the Bristol Channel when the towline snapped. The ship's rudder had broken, and the crew could no longer steer it. In desperation they had lowered the anchors, hoping to prevent the ship from bashing into the rocks along the shore. For now the anchors were holding, but the *Forrest Hall* was at the mercy of the gale.

The steep incline from Lynmouth up Countisbury Hill is shown here. The journey from Lynmouth to a better launching place was 14 miles.

In the village, the telegram was rushed to Jack Crocombe, the sailor who was in charge of the Lynmouth lifeboat, the *Louisa*. The lifeboat crew was quickly summoned. Within minutes, fourteen shivering men clad in oilskin raincoats were gathered at the lifeboat house beside the harbor.

Quickly they discussed the situation. Launching their boat would be impossible. The coast was jagged and lined with rocks and steep cliffs. The waves were too rough. The *Louisa* would be smashed to pieces.

"We'll launch from Porlock."

Then inspiration struck Jack. He knew the coastline well. There was one town nearby that had a sheltered cove. It would be safe to launch the *Louisa* from there.

"We'll launch from Porlock," he told the men.

Some thought him crazy. Porlock? In *this* weather?

It did seem impossible. To launch *Louisa*, a 4-ton wooden rowboat, at Porlock meant a 14-mile overland journey along narrow mountain roads, around tight curves, up steep hills, and down dangerous inclines. Even in sunny, dry conditions it would be a daunting task. In a gale like this, at night, it just didn't seem possible.

But the more the men talked, the more they realized that Jack's plan was the only hope for the *Forrest Hall*. The lives of its eighteen crew were in danger. Lynmouth had lost sailors and ships of its own in conditions like this. The men gathered in the boathouse that night had strong ties to the sea and knew the hazards of stormy weather, the perils of rocks and thrashing waves. Without their help, the ship would likely snap its moorings, drift into the rocks, and break apart.

The villagers had to act. And soon. "To Porlock," they agreed.

Jack's plan was the only hope for the *Forrest Hall.*

The call for help spread through the village. Men and women arrived, oil lanterns in hand, ready to face the storm and help the crew of the *Forrest Hall*. Together they hoisted the *Louisa* onto its carriage and tied it down. A team of twenty horses was secured to pull it. At 8 P.M. they started for Porlock, horses straining, some villagers pulling with ropes, others pushing from behind.

The first stretch of the journey was the worst — over 2 miles up steep Countisbury Hill. Bucking the wind and driving rain, they towed the carriage up the road. Partway a wheel fell off. With everyone's help the carriage was lifted, the wheel reattached, and the pushing and pulling resumed. Hours later they arrived at the top of the hill, 1,000 feet above Lynmouth.

The rest of the journey would be along level grades or downhill. Soaking wet and tired, some villagers left and returned home. They figured fewer hands were needed for the remainder of the journey. Twenty men continued with the *Louisa*.

The mountain road was rutted and slick with mud. Four miles farther along, it thinned. The carriage was too wide to pass. The *Louisa* was unloaded, lowered onto wooden skids, and dragged. Only a few yards could be managed at a time. Then the men would have to stop, pick up the skids behind the boat, carry them to the front, reposition them on the road, and start again. And so it went. Drag the *Louisa* a few yards. Stop. Reposition the skids. Drag some more.

Meanwhile the carriage was hauled by horses across the open field to bypass the narrow section of road. When the *Louisa* finally met up with the carriage, she was hoisted back aboard.

The tugging and towing continued. To get to the harbor at Porlock, the men had to roll the carriage down a long, sharp incline. Drag chains were fastened to the back of the carriage to slow it down. Horses were untethered from the front and hitched to the rear. Ropes were attached to the back, double knotted, and secured. Straining against the load, men and horses rolled the carriage down the muddy road, around one tight turn after another.

There were obstacles—a section of road had been washed out in the storm, a garden wall was too near, a tree stood in the way. The men of Lynmouth bypassed the washed-out section, demolished the garden wall, and chopped down the tree.

By the time they reached the bottom of Porlock Hill, it was 6 o'clock in the morning, ten hours since they'd left Lynmouth. Tired, hungry, and cold, they refused to give up. The men hauled the boat across the beach. Ten of them took their stations on the *Louisa* and launched her into the wind-tossed sea.

After a night of hauling the lifeboat over land, the men rowed for an hour more in the stormy sea to reach the *Forrest Hall*. When they finally got to the ship, they found that its anchors had held. The frightened crew was still safe . . . for the moment. But the seas were too rough to attempt a rescue.

"We'll stand by," Jack shouted, bringing hope to the stricken crew. Stationing themselves nearby, the *Louisa* and her weary crew watched over the *Forrest Hall*, ready to save the men should the anchors fail. When a tugboat finally arrived, men from the *Louisa* boarded the *Forrest Hall* to lend a hand. The *Louisa* accompanied the two ships the final stretch. Just in case the line snapped, they would be there.

It was 5 o'clock that evening when the vessels finally arrived at the port town of Barry. Almost a full day had passed since the call for help had come in. The Lynmouth men were exhausted and shivering, their stomachs empty. After a change of clothes and a satisfying meal, they crawled into warm beds provided by the grateful folk of Barry.

The next day the seas were calm. The *Louisa* and her crew were towed back to Lynmouth, heroes to the cheering crowd that had gathered on the dock there, the stuff of legend for coming generations.

A full century later, on January 12, 1999, the town of Lynmouth celebrated the famous launch in a special way. Using a replica of the *Louisa* they reenacted the rescue, hauling her up and down the same steep hills, and around the same sharp curves as their courageous ancestors.

*For two families, the dream of freedom far
outweighed their fears.*

FLOATING TO
FREEDOM

In a ground-floor gallery of the Wall Museum in Berlin,
Germany, sits a basketlike frame made of metal, wood,
and clothesline. The basket was once part of something
larger — a homemade hot-air balloon. Looking at it now,
it's hard to believe that anyone would dare ride in something so unstable. Yet someone did, and not just one
person, but eight desperate people. Two entire families,
in fact.

The basket, like the entire Wall Museum, reminds
visitors of the time before 1989 when Germany was
divided in two — on one side Communist-controlled
East Germany, on the other West Germany, a demo-
cratically run country. Separating the two countries
was a heavily fortified 858-mile-long border that prevented the citizens of East Germany from freely entering West Germany. Guarding the border were 10- to
13-foot-high metal fences, coils of razor-sharp barbed
wire, and watchtowers equipped with searchlights and

sirens, manned by East German soldiers with orders to shoot anyone trying to flee. Of the entire system, the Berlin Wall, a concrete barrier separating the cities of East and West Berlin, is the most famous section, though it formed less than a tenth of the structure.

Yet despite the dangers, freedom remained a tantalizing dream for many East Germans. Some tried to escape by scaling the border fence, by digging tunnels underneath, or by sneaking across border checkpoints by hiding in cars. A few were successful. Hundreds were captured or shot.

For Peter Strelczyk and his neighbor Gunter Wetzel, talk of escape from East Germany was constant. One day in 1978, while watching a television program on the history of ballooning, they had an idea. Why not build a hot-air balloon, float it over the border, and escape by air instead of on foot? It seemed outrageous, an unlikely plan if ever there was one, yet somehow it felt possible.

Though Peter had been a mechanic, neither knew much about ballooning. They started by visiting the library and reading what they could. Armed with a notepad, Peter made a few calculations. The balloon would have to be large enough to carry eight passengers—both men plus their families. Factoring in the weight of the passengers, basket, fabric, burner, cylinders of fuel, and other equipment, Peter estimated the total load to be roughly 1,700 pounds. To lift that much, a huge balloon would be needed—one capable of holding 99,000 cubic feet of air.

In secret, they started construction. To obtain the 9,500 square feet of fabric they needed, Peter and Gunter shopped around East Germany, buying rolls of material here and bedsheets there. In the Wetzels' attic they cut the fabric into triangles and rectangles, and sewed the pieces together on an old, foot-operated sewing machine. Propane bottles rigged to a stovepipe became the burner. For the basket Peter welded a metal frame. Wooden boards became the floor. A clothesline strung between the corners served as a guardrail.

To avoid suspicion the two men went to their jobs every day, just as usual. But afterward they worked long into the night on their balloon. Several weeks later they had a finished product—a 50-foot-wide, 65-foot-high patchwork balloon complete with makeshift basket and burner. To test it they hauled it to a forest clearing in the dead of night, fired up a blower to push air into the balloon, started the burners . . . and prayed.

There were failures and setbacks. Their first balloon leaked, which meant starting over using airtight material. Then, just when it seemed they had all the bugs ironed out of the system, the Wetzels backed out. The escape plan was too risky, they felt, the chance of getting caught too high.

Disappointed but not beaten, the Strelczyks forged ahead on their own. With the balloon packed and ready,

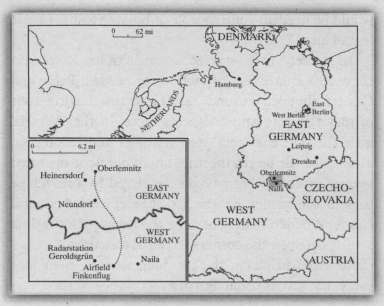

Germany was divided into East and West, with the city of Berlin—also divided—surrounded by East Germany. The inset (left) shows the escapees' route.

they waited for perfect weather—a night free of rain with a light wind to push them over the border.

On July 3, 1979, conditions were near perfect. Wearing warm clothes, the Strelczyks drove with the balloon and basket to the forest clearing. Peter started up the blower, and the balloon swelled in size until it towered above the trees. The family scrambled aboard.

The launch was gentle and steady. Within minutes they were soaring at 6,200 feet, drifting with the wind toward the West German border. Then the balloon passed through clouds. The fabric sucked up water droplets and gained weight. The balloon dropped slowly, clipped treetops, dropped some more, then plowed into the ground.

Today the homemade hot-air balloon is exhibited in the Mauermuseum-Museum Haus am Checkpoint Charlie (Wall Museum) in Berlin, Germany.

The Strelczyks were unharmed, but were they in West Germany? They scoured the area with a flashlight. On the ground near a wire fence was a torn package that read "People's Owned Bakery, Wernigerode." The wording told them that they were still in East Germany, a few hundred yards short of the border.

Forced to leave the balloon behind, the Strelczyks headed home, disappointed but more convinced than ever that escape in a hot-air balloon was entirely possible. They would start over, they decided. Buy more fabric and quickly build another balloon, for there was no time to lose — their abandoned balloon would eventually be found. Soon the East German police would be on their trail, asking questions, searching for clues.

They were still in East Germany, a few hundred yards short of the border.

Hearing of the plans for a new balloon, the Wetzels decided to take part. Together the two families combed East Germany for more fabric. By working in shifts, they had a new, larger balloon finished within two weeks.

Again they waited for perfect weather. It finally arrived on the night of September 16, 1979. They drove to the launch site and set up quickly. Standing shoulder to shoulder on the platform, they cut the ropes anchoring the balloon. It rose above the trees and was pushed toward the West German border by a gentle wind.

As the balloon neared the border, searchlights caught it. Would the soldiers open fire? Peter gave the flame a boost, shooting the balloon higher. Below, they could make out houses, headlights of vehicles moving on streets, and then, as they continued to drift, open fields and trees.

The flame flickered, coughed, and sputtered. They were running out of fuel. The balloon slowly dropped. Then, 16 feet above ground, the gas gave out completely. They thudded into a blackberry bush, which left them breathless, but unhurt.

The entire flight had lasted twenty-eight minutes. Had it got them over the border?

Peter and Gunter explored the area. Their surroundings looked no different than those they would see in East Germany. Then a car approached—an Audi, a western-made vehicle. There were two men inside the car and the word POLICE was painted on its side.

"Are we in West Germany?" Peter asked.

The policemen nodded. Immediately, Peter and Gunter embraced them in a hug, shouting "We made it! We made it!"

And they had. Two families, eight people in all, had escaped from East Germany to West Germany. They had risked their lives to travel from Communism to democracy—all in a flimsy, homemade balloon.

*The passengers and crew of Flight 93 were
powerless to stop the hijackers. Or were they?*

FLIGHT 93

No one knows the full story of Flight 93. No one
survived the flight, and without living witnesses to
testify, the story has to be reassembled from phone messages left by passengers, words captured on the cockpit
voice recorder, and exchanges between crew and the
ground.

This much we know: United Airlines Flight 93 was
forty-one minutes late leaving New Jersey on the morning of September 11, 2001. The Boeing 757 sat on the
tarmac — thirty-seven passengers, five flight attendants,
and two pilots — waiting for clearance to depart for San
Francisco. After receiving the go-ahead, the plane rumbled down the runway at 8:42 A.M. By 9:00 A.M. Flight 93
was cruising at an altitude of 31,000 feet and reaching
speeds of 500 miles per hour.

Flight attendants served coffee and breakfast. Passengers relaxed. Some used Airfones on the back of seats to
place calls to relatives or friends. Others read or slept.

Roughly forty minutes after takeoff, air traffic con-
trollers in Cleveland heard voices in the cockpit. "Hey,
get out of here," someone said.

That was followed by a second voice with a thick Arabic accent making an announcement to passengers. "Please sit down. Keep remaining seating. We have a bomb on board, so sit."

Evidence gathered after the fact suggests that there were four hijackers among the passengers. The leader, Ziad Jarrah, was twenty-six years old, trained in martial arts, with experience flying planes. The others, also in their twenties, were full of zeal and fiery conviction, and willing to do anything for their cause.

The hijackers waited until the plane had reached cruising speed, then pulled red bandanas around their heads and took control of the plane. Armed with knives, one guarded the first-class section while two others forced their way into the cockpit. One hijacker grabbed the loudspeaker microphone to deliver the message. In the scuffle, they stabbed two people, likely the pilot and copilot. Twenty-seven passengers and crew were herded into the coach section at the rear of the plane.

Between 9:31 and 10:01 A.M., passengers and crew members made frantic phone calls to friends and loved ones from the coach section — twenty-three calls from the seat-back phones alone, and still others from cell phones carried aboard. Stitched together, the phone calls tell much of what is known about the struggle aboard Flight 93.

Tom Burnett was one of the first passengers to place a call. "We are in the air," he told his wife, Deena, who was at home in California. "The hijackers have already knifed a guy. They are telling us there is a bomb on board. Please call the authorities."

Joseph Deluca, on his way to San Francisco for vacation, called his father and said, "The plane's been hijacked." Then he added, "I love you."

Flight attendant CeeCee Lyles phoned her husband, Lorne, in Fort Myers, Florida, and left a message on the answering machine. She prayed for her family and herself. "I hope I'll see your face again," she said.

When Tom Burnett called Deena again, she told him what everyone on the ground already knew. The World Trade Center in New York had been slammed into by two planes and was in flames. "They are hijacking planes all up and down the east coast. They are taking them and hitting designated targets," Deena told Tom.

Word about the World Trade Center spread among the passengers. There was talk, too, that a third plane had hit the Pentagon in Washington.

Somewhere outside Cleveland, Flight 93 made a sharp turn. "Okay! We're going down!" Todd Beamer said in his call to Lisa Jefferson, a supervisor with Airfone. "No, we're okay. I think we're turning around."

Around that time, talk aboard Flight 93 took on a different tone. Were the hijackers part of the same terrorist plot? Were they going to crash their plane, too? In the coach section, passengers and crew held whispered

Investigators at the Flight 93 crash site in Pennsylvania.

discussions. There was mention of a takeover, an uprising against the hijackers.

"We're waiting until we're over a rural area. We're going to take back the airplane," Tom Burnett said in his last call, just before 10 A.M. "Pray, just pray, Deena."

Passenger Jeremy Glick told his wife that they were going to take a vote.

Flight attendant Sandy Bradshaw said to her husband that they were going to rush the hijackers. She was boiling water to throw on them. She also mentioned something else. "I see a river." Though Sandy couldn't name it, the information suggested that Flight 93 was somewhere over western Pennsylvania.

Todd Beamer mentioned a plan in his call to Lisa Jefferson. He said that the passengers were going to storm the aisle to the first-class cabin and attack the hijacker there. "Are you ready?" Lisa heard him say to someone else. "Okay. Let's roll."

Honor Wainio was on the line with her stepmother. "I need to go," she said. "They're getting ready to break into the cockpit. I love you. Good-bye."

At 9:54 A.M. the plane lost altitude and started flying erratically. At 9:57 A.M. the flight recorder began picking up the sounds of screams and shouts, bangs and crashes, breaking glass, cockpit alarms, and rushes of wind.

"In the cockpit. If we don't, we die."

Experts who have analyzed the recording believe this was when the passengers and crew made their move. Some theorize that a food cart was used to rush down the aisle and bash the cockpit door, but whatever the weapon, there is little question that a sustained assault was made by Flight 93's passengers and crew. Realizing that the plane they were on would become an instrument of destruction, they fought to regain control.

The cockpit recorder verifies this. In one of the last taped exchanges, a passenger is heard shouting, "In the cockpit. If we don't, we die." Moments later, a voice says, "Roll it."

The temporary memorial overlooking the crash site where visitors left personal items, flowers, and notes.

Groans follow, screams, thuds, static, cries of pain. A hijacker shouts, "Allah is the greatest. Allah is the greatest," over and over.

On the phone, Lorne Lyles heard CeeCee scream, "They're doing it! They're doing it! They're doing it!" Then the line went dead.

At 10:03 A.M. Flight 93 slammed into a Pennsylvania field, digging a crater into the ground, instantly killing all on board. There is speculation that Flight 93 was aiming for the White House, and that Ziad Jarrah purposely crashed the jet when his plans were foiled. There seems no doubt that the passengers and crew were responsible. By taking action they thwarted a plan of destruction that would have cost many more lives.

> *"Somehow the brave men and women on Flight 93, knowing they would die, found the courage to use their final moments to save the lives of others. . . . Few are called to show the kind of valor seen on Flight 93, or on the field of battle. Yet all of us do share a calling: Be strong in adversity and unafraid in danger."*
>
> — U.S. PRESIDENT GEORGE W. BUSH

CALLED TO ACTION | **September 5, 1986 / Karachi, Pakistan**

When Palestinian terrorists rushed a Pan Am jet waiting on the tarmac at Karachi's ariport, flight attendant Neerja Bhanot was one of the first to notice. She shouted "Hijack!" and alerted the flight crew to the situation. Immediately they escaped, leaving the plane pilotless and upsetting the terrorists' plan of flying the plane to Cypress and using it to secure the release of Palestinian prisoners being held there. Forced to remain on the tarmac, hijackers held 379 terrified passengers and crew hostage for the next seventeen hours.

Throughout the ordeal, Neerja did what she could to ensure the safety and comfort of those on board. When ordered to hand over the passports of U.S. passengers, Neerja hid them instead. Then when the frustrated hijackers opened fire, attempting to kill as many passengers as possible, she threw open one of the emergency doors. Rather than being the first to exit, she pushed people down the chute and used her body as a protective shield. Neerja died trying to save three children. Although twenty-one people lost their lives, without her steely courage the death toll would have been much higher.

For her heroic actions that day, Neerja Bhanot was posthumously awarded the U.S. Special Courage Award, as well as the Ashoka Chakra, India's highest honor for bravery.

Caught in a flooded Pennsylvania mine, nine men made a pact — they would live or die together.

NINE MEN TOGETHER

Deep below Somerset, Pennsylvania, in 2002, nine miners toiled in the heart of Quecreek Mine, chipping rock, loading coal, and shuttling it to the surface. It was backbreaking work, but to the men in the tunnel there was no other life. For some, it was what their fathers and grandfathers before them had done, too.

The nine men were like brothers, so close they had nicknames for each other. Mark Popernack was Moe, and that night, just two hours from the end of the shift, he was operating the continuous miner, a machine that pulverized rock into manageable pieces. The rest were doing other jobs: bolting new sections of roof in place to secure the tunnel, scooping up debris, or loading coal onto the conveyor belt for transport to the surface.

It was a normal shift until around quarter to nine, when the continuous miner pierced a wall of rock and broke into an abandoned mine containing

150 million gallons of water—enough to fill more than 225 Olympic-size swimming pools. Immediately there was a gusher.

Thomas "Tucker" Foy noticed the water first. "Everyone out!" he yelled. But before there was time to react, the hole widened and water exploded into the tunnel.

"Harpo! Get out, now!" Popernack screamed to Dennis Hall, who was behind him, operating a shuttle car loaded with coal. Safe from the flood but cut off from the others by the water, Popernack yelled at them to run and save themselves. The men scattered.

Hall, meanwhile, drove the heavy, electric-powered shuttle car down the tunnel, racing to stay ahead of the water. He managed 100 feet before the vehicle was swamped. Ditching it, Hall ran to the phone and placed an urgent call to miners working in the other side of the mine. "Get out!" he screamed when someone picked up the phone. "Get out! You've got major water!" Then he joined the others at Entry 4, where the conveyor belt that stretched the length of the mine and transported coal to the surface was located. In the dark it was difficult to see how the shafts and passageways that crisscrossed the tunnel connected, or to tell which ones were already filling with water. The miners knew the conveyor belt led upwards and, even though water had cut its power, they pinned their hopes on reaching the surface with it.

"Get out! You've got major water!"

Crouching low, they crept along beside the conveyor, their headlamps lighting the way, water up to their necks. Eventually, to speed up their progress, they hopped onto the conveyor belt and crawled over the coal on it, bloodying their knuckles and scraping their knees.

Hope was strong. Then, 2,600 feet along the belt, they saw the glimmer of water ahead, a sign their plan had failed. Water was backing into the tunnels, cutting off their chance to escape.

"Turn around," the men in the lead yelled.

Water lapped at their chins as they fought to crawl back before the tunnel filled completely. Their only chance to survive was to return to Entry 4 and find a high place inside the mine that was still dry.

"Get me over with you guys!" he yelled.

Popernack, meanwhile, was alone. He was caught on one side of the tunnel, separated from the others by water pouring from the breached wall. Suddenly he saw the headlamp of one of the returning miners.

"Get me over with you guys!" he yelled.

When the gusher slowed slightly, Randy Fogle, the crew chief, jumped aboard a scooper machine, raised the bucket, and drove it into the water. "Jump!" he yelled.

Popernack leaped into the bucket and Fogle reversed directions.

The men were together again, all nine. They vowed to stay that way, for good or for bad, no matter the cost.

The men knew the ways of the mine, and this gave them hope and also a plan. They knew that Hall's phone call would have started a chain reaction. Police, paramedics, firefighters, and rescue squads would have been alerted. By now, mine officials would be discussing ways of getting them out. Maps of the mine would be unfurled, diagrams studied, experts consulted — geologists, surveyors, divers, drillers, anyone with knowledge of rocks or coal or water. They would figure out where the miners were, then find some way of drilling twenty-four stories down through solid rock to bring them back to the surface.

For the nine men, water was the enemy, but so was time. In the cold, wet mine, hypothermia was a real threat. So was the challenge of finding enough oxygen. The longer the men were below, the slimmer their chance of survival. At best, rescue was a long shot. But miracles do happen, the miners told themselves, and they could help this one along by staying together in one spot and doing whatever they could to stay alive until they were found.

They started by building a dike at Entry 4 using

cinder blocks left lying in the tunnel. The dike would shield them from rising water and give them a chance to survive, or at least allow them to be together if they died. By the light of their headlamps they hauled blocks, passed them to each other, and stacked them high. Chilled by the water and with oxygen levels steadily dropping, it was bone-numbing, exhausting work.

At best, rescue was a long shot.

Some time after 3 A.M., six hours after the breach began, they heard a sound — the drone of a distant drill somewhere in the mine. The sound was getting closer. Help was coming, they knew, and this renewed their flagging spirits.

At 5:10 A.M., eight hours after the breach first began, a 6-inch drill punctured the roof of Entry 4. A steel pipe dropped into sight. The miners tapped it three times to send a message to the surface. Then they waited, and tapped it again, nine times more. Nine men together, nine men alive, their message said.

Warm, oxygen-rich air flowed into the tunnel where the miners were. With rescue a possibility, they worked harder, stacking blocks, building walls. Still the water rose. By noon on Thursday, they were forced to flee to higher ground.

Tucker figured they had an hour until the water reached them. An hour before they drowned. They wrote messages to loved ones, stuffed them into a plastic bucket, and strapped it to a boulder. Afterward they looped steel cable through their miner belts, connecting themselves one to the other. If they died, it would be as a team. Their bodies would be found together.

They shared tears, prayers, last good-byes . . . and waited. An hour passed. The water still hadn't reached them and a quick check showed that it had stopped rising. Up above, rescuers had gotten pumps working to stem the flow of water into the mine. Far off, they could hear the sound of drilling.

They shared tears, prayers, last good-byes . . . and waited.

The miners switched to a new plan. Rescue was quickly becoming a reality. It wouldn't be long now, they thought, untying themselves. They shut off their headlamps to conserve energy, sat back-to-back to retain heat, hugged those wracked with shivers, and when spirits sagged, rallied each other with a bit of cheer—a joke, a memory, a dream of the future. They kept up the pounding, too. Nine taps on the rocky ceiling. Nine men still alive. Keep drilling.

Hours crawled along. Thursday turned into Friday. Then at 1:50 A.M., twenty-nine hours after the gusher had started, the drilling stopped and an eerie silence took over.

They've given up on us, the miners thought. "Not so," said Fogle. "They must have broken a bit, that's all."

And so they hung on a while longer and worked out another plan. As the water level dropped, every ten or fifteen minutes they took turns walking in pairs 250 feet down the passageway to pound nine times on the metal pipe.

Nine men alive. Please don't give up on us.

Time passed slowly. The miners kept up their visits to the pipe and their nine-times pounding, but for fourteen hours all they heard was silence. Slowly their enthusiasm sagged. Then on Friday around 8 P.M., almost forty-eight hours after the start of the disaster, they heard it again—the drone of a drill chewing through rock, steady and loud.

At 10:15 P.M. on Saturday, it was Thomas Foy and Roy Hileman's turn to make the journey down the passageway to the pipe. The lights on their headlamps were dim, and the men were weak and cold.

On the way, they found a surprise. There was a new hole, a shaft wider than a person in the tunnel ceiling, one that hadn't been there before. "We found the hole!" Hileman screamed. "Everyone get down there!"

After 77 hours trapped underground, a miner is brought to the surface in a rescue capsule.

They ran. At the hole, they yelled and tapped to send a message. A cage was lowered to take the miners home. First up was Randy Fogle, who broke the surface at 12:55 A.M. on Sunday amid cheers and wild celebration. He was followed by the rest, one by one, each fifteen minutes apart—Moe, Tucker, Harpo, and the others. Their faces, black with coal dust, bore broad smiles. Cold and shivering, they had beaten the odds. They were safe now, the ordeal over, nine men together.

> *"Everybody had strong moments. Maybe one guy got down, then the rest pulled together. Then that guy would get up and someone else would feel a little weaker. It was a team effort: That's the only way it could have been."*

— HARRY MAYHUGH

CALLED TO ACTION | **October 23, 1958 / Nova Scotia, Canada**

When a section of the Springhill Number 2 Mine collapsed, tunnels were flattened and dozens of miners killed instantly. Others were trapped.

The Springhill mines had a long history of problems. In 1891 an explosion had rocked the mine, killing 125 men, and making it Canada's worst mining disaster ever. In 1956 another explosion took the lives of 39 more. With these tragic memories in place, off-duty miners and rescuers scrambled to the Number 2 mine on October 23, 1958, knowing that survival for those trapped below depended on quick action.

Among those trapped in complete darkness was Maurice Ruddick. With him were six other men. They were in a small pocket deep within the mine, 13,000 feet below the surface. No one on the surface knew their location, or if they were even alive. As hours edged into days, hope among the men faded.

Maurice, however, had a cheerful outlook on life and an excellent singing voice. To keep the miners' spirits high, he entertained them with songs, told jokes, and even organized a birthday party for one of the men on the fourth day. In private, though, he kept his worries tightly contained. "I cried quietly in the darkness, but I made sure nobody else heard me," he said later. "It might have broken their resolve to live."

CALLED TO ACTION **October 23, 1958 / Nova Scotia, Canada**

On the ninth day, when rescuers finally broke into the tomb, they found Maurice still singing. "Give me a drink of water and I'll sing you a song," he told them.

Modestly, Maurice maintained that he had done nothing special, but the other miners disagreed. He had kept up their spirits in their darkest hour.

He had been one of the lucky ones, Terry Fox thought. Now it was time to do something for others.

TERRY'S MIRACLE

For Terry Fox, September 1, 1980, started much the same as the 143 days before. He woke up in darkness, donned shorts and a T-shirt printed with a map of Canada, strapped on his artificial leg, and, after a few stretches to limber up his aching muscles, hit the road. Followed by a beige van driven by his best friend, Doug Alward, Terry ran down the Trans-Canada Highway, starting yet another day of his Marathon of Hope run across Canada.

On this dull, drizzly day northeast of Thunder Bay, Ontario, Terry was 3,339 miles from St. John's, Newfoundland, his starting point, and two-thirds of the way to Vancouver, British Columbia, his final destination. The twenty-two-year-old was running his dream, raising money to fight cancer, the disease that had taken his leg four years before.

Like so many previous days, Terry started strong and confident. He fell into a familiar rhythm, his left leg thumping double time on the pavement, his fiberglass and steel one thunking in return. He didn't know yet that the day would be his last spent running, or that, as dreams often go, his would morph into something new — something larger, grander, and longer-lasting than the original.

The cancer had caught him by surprise. It had started as a sharp pain in his right knee when he was in his first year of Physical Education at Simon Fraser University, a stone's throw from his home in Port Coquitlam, a district of Vancouver. Then one morning Terry found that he couldn't stand. That pushed him to see a doctor.

Terry was told he had osteogenic sarcoma, a form of bone cancer. To save his life, the leg had to be amputated 6 inches above the knee. His chances of survival were 50 to 70 percent — two years earlier his chances would have been just 15 percent. In those two years, there had been advances in treatment, new methods, improved drugs — all of which spelled hope for Terry.

The evening before his operation, Terry read a magazine article about an amputee who had run the New York Marathon, and a seed was planted.

After surgery Terry had to endure sixteen months of painful treatment. At the clinic he saw the pain and suffering of other cancer victims. For many, the chance of survival was slim. Only one-third of patients made it.

When he left the clinic fitted with his prosthetic leg,

assured that his body was rid of cancer—at least for now—Terry carried the burden of what he had seen. He'd been lucky, he realized. Not everyone who had cancer was. He could do something about it. He could change those odds. He should, too.

"I could not leave knowing these faces and feelings would still exist even though I would be set free from mine," Terry wrote later. "Somewhere the hurting must stop."

And that's where the idea for the Marathon of Hope was born. Terry resolved to run across Canada and raise $1 million for cancer research. It was a wild and improbable goal—a single person, an amputee at that, still weak from treatment, running through wind and rain across one of the world's largest countries, collecting pledges for the miles he ran. But rather than being discouraged by the enormity of the task, Terry saw it as an opportunity.

"I'm a dreamer," he said. "I like challenges. I don't give up. When I decided to do it, I knew I was going to go all out. There was no in between."

He started training immediately, first in his wheelchair. Finding the steepest, roughest trails around Vancouver, Terry pushed himself until his hands were raw. A few months later he switched to running.

His new leg took some getting used to. When he stumbled and crashed, as Terry often did at first, he dusted himself off and started again. Finding the right stride

Terry Fox in Montreal, Quebec.

took time. Slowly he gained the stability and strength to make it work. After fifteen months of training, after logging more than 3,000 miles, Terry could run 26 miles in a single stretch. He was ready.

By now, Terry had raised the stakes of his goal. A million dollars seemed small. He saw the marathon in larger terms, involving people from around the country. After the ten thousand people of Port aux Basques, Newfoundland, raised $10,000, Terry vowed to raise $1 for every person living in Canada — $22 million.

Terry approached the Canadian Cancer Society and discussed his plan. To his surprise the reception was lukewarm. Believing his goal was unrealistic, administrators told him to find corporate support, secure pledges, and contact them again when he had stronger proof that he was serious about it.

Terry did just that. He composed a passionate letter requesting support for his run. "The running I can do," he wrote, "even if I have to crawl every last mile. We need your help. The people in cancer clinics all over the world need people who believe in miracles."

In a few months Terry returned to the Cancer Society, pledges in hand, and finally received the backing he needed.

On April 12, 1980, Terry dipped his artificial leg in St. John's Harbour on Canada's east coast to kick off the start of his run. Every day afterward—windy, rainy, cold, or unbearably hot—Terry ran, fists clenched, jaw set, eyes locked on the horizon. He wound his way across the Maritimes, through Quebec and into Ontario, coming closer to Vancouver with every step.

Terry kept a journal during his journey. It was a place to record thoughts and impressions, good times and bad. In early July, just outside of Ottawa, he wrote: "Everybody seems to have given up hope of trying. I haven't. It isn't easy and it isn't supposed to be, but I'm accomplishing something. How many people give up a lot to do something good? I'm sure we would have found a cure for cancer twenty years ago if we had really tried."

Word spread about the curly-haired young man and his impossible goal. Donations small and large began pouring in — a dollar here, a thousand there. Radio and television broadcasters gave updates on his progress. Bystanders lined the route, pressed money into his hand, gave him hugs, cheered him on. His run became their run, his cause their own.

On the morning of September 1, 1980, as he began his run just outside Thunder Bay, Terry felt the same enthusiasm as usual. There was pain, too, of course — the chafing of his raw stump in the saddle of his prosthesis; the throbbing jolt the leg made as it impacted the pavement. Those were pains he felt every day. But that drizzly day there was another pain. It was in Terry's chest, deep and stabbing, a pain newer than the others. There was a persistent cough as well. It hung around and no amount of determination could make it go away.

He knew he couldn't outrun it this time.

Like always, Terry ignored the pain and kept his thoughts on his goal. He'd gotten through a lot of pain in the past four years. He'd get through this new bout in the same way. But he couldn't. After a few miles, it became harder to breathe. He felt his energy drain, his body slacken and grow weak, the pain in his chest deepen. He knew he couldn't outrun it this time.

People lined the highway. A few stood in silent awe, entranced by the sight of the champion. Some clapped. Others shouted encouragement. "Keep going, don't give up, you can do it, you can make it, we're all behind you."

Not wanting to let them down, Terry put on a brave face and plodded on, past a camera crew filming him, past a curve in the road. Once out of sight, he pulled over and crawled inside the van. "Take me to the hospital," he told Doug Alward.

The diagnosis wasn't good. Cancer had spread to his lungs. "I'm going to do my very best. I'll fight, I promise I won't give up," Terry told reporters at a press conference. "This just intensifies what I did. It gives it more meaning. It'll inspire more people.... When I started this run, I said that if we all gave $1, we'd have $22 million for cancer research, and I don't care, man, there's no reason that isn't possible. No reason."

Terry was flown to a Vancouver hospital. While he struggled with the disease, the rest of Canada took on his cause. A Canadian businessman pledged to hold a fund-raising run each year for cancer research in Terry's name. A television network held a special five-hour telethon and raised $10 million. In the following months, more donations were received. In the end, a

Terry Fox ran a total of 3,159 miles during his training
for the Marathon of Hope. The image of him pounding out
such grueling distances, day after day, has inspired
hundreds of thousands of people to enter the annual
Terry Fox Run in their own communities.

total of $24.17 million was raised for cancer research, surpassing Terry's goal.

Terry, meanwhile, continued his battle with cancer. From his hospital bed, he laid the ground rules for future fund-raising runs. He wanted them to be non-competitive — no awards, no winners or losers, just everyday people joined in the pursuit of a common goal: finding a cure for cancer.

Terry died on June 28, 1981, one month short of his twenty-third birthday. His legacy lives on, however. Every September the Terry Fox Run (National School Run Day and Terry Fox Works Day) is held in cities and towns across Canada and around the world. Hundreds of thousands of people participate, running, walking, biking, or rollerblading to raise money for cancer research. To date more than $400 million has been collected for cancer research. There have been major advances in cancer treatment, too, and the chances of recovery have steadily improved.

CALLED TO ACTION   April, 1995 / Thornhill, Ontario

When twelve-year-old Craig Kielburger read a newspaper article about Iqbal Masih, a young boy from Pakistan who had been sold into slavery to work in a carpet factory, he knew he had to do something. Iqbal had been murdered when he began speaking out about children's rights. Troubled by the story, Craig gathered eleven school friends and started Free the Children, an organization of children helping children. He journeyed around the globe, speaking publicly, drawing attention to the plight of the world's unfortunate children, and challenging young people to make a difference. Today Free the Children is the world's largest youth network, involving over one million young people from forty-five countries.

CALLED TO ACTION   World War II / Le Chambon, France

The village of Le Chambon sits high in the mountains of southern France. During World War II it was the scene of a quiet revolution. Led by Andre Trocmé, the young pastor of a Protestant church there, and his wife, Magda, the villagers of Le Chambon banded together to oppose the Nazi regime. When Jews who were fleeing for their lives showed up on their doorsteps, the villagers hid them in their homes and schools, treated them like family, and provided them with food, clothing, and

CALLED TO ACTION	World War II / Le Chambon, France

protection. When possible, they obtained travel documents and arranged safe passage to more trouble-free countries like Switzerland or Spain.

The villagers of tiny Le Chambon did this under the careful watch of the enemy, using clever tactics to avoid detection. If, for example, French gendarmes or German Gestapo arrived to inspect the village, the residents sent the refugees into the hills and forest to hide. They adopted a system of signals. Closed shutters on the windows of a home meant soldiers were searching the house. Shutters opened again meant they were gone, and it was safe to return.

During the four years that France was occupied, the villagers of Le Chambon rescued five thousand Jewish refugees without lifting a weapon, without shedding blood, by hiding complete strangers for days, sometimes even years. They did it together, a community united, never once turning away, denouncing, or betraying a single person.

For their courageous actions, the villagers of Le Chambon have been honored with the title Righteous Among the Nations by Yad Vashem, an Israeli group charged with documenting and preserving memories of the Holocaust period.

EPILOGUE

The people in these stories had difficult decisions to make. What was behind their choices? What motivated them to act as they did, to select one path over another?

For some, like Erica Pratt, Jillian Searle, and Simon Yates, survival forced their hand. Do something now or you might die. And so they did. Erica defied a threat of death if she tried to escape. Jillian passed one of her sons to a bystander so they might all survive. Believing his climbing buddy was likely dead, Simon cut the rope. It was the only way to get himself off the mountain alive, he figured. Even if we don't agree with their choices, there is something admirable about their actions. These people fought panic and fear and conquered it with calmness and fierce determination.

In some cases, survival required a group effort. The Quecreek miners banded together, giving each other the support they needed to keep their hopes alive until they could all be rescued. Michael Mayen, too, felt the support and friendship of his companions. Traveling as a group, with safety in numbers, he and many other Lost Boys survived what seems like an impossible journey. In these situations, trust and loyalty created an undefeatable bond.

Something other than physical survival, though, was involved in other stories. How else can we explain Tank

Man's decision to put personal safety aside and step in front of a moving tank? Consider, too, the daring action taken by the Strelczyk and Wetzel families—eight people, fleeing a Communist-run country in a home-made hot-air balloon. And what of Marina Nemat's defiant acts in school? She knew that to speak out against the government would have serious outcomes. These people were driven by a different kind of survival—the survival of rights and freedom. Backed into a corner by political circumstances, they could not stand idly by. They had to step forward and do or say something—whatever the consequences.

There were those whose decisions, though, seemed guided by something else. When trouble broke out, Chuck Pelletier went back to Hotel Orchid to check on his friends. Six-year-old Deamonte Love herded the toddlers in his care down Causeway Boulevard, all the while keeping the promise he'd made his mother. With the tip of Everest in sight, Andrew Brash gave up the dream of a lifetime to help Lincoln Hall. These people seemed driven by an inner code, a sense of right and wrong that made their choices clear and the path of action well defined. Friendship, honor, and the needs of others played heavily in their decisions.

We could say the same of the villagers of Lynmouth who launched an impossible rescue to save strangers in a wild storm. Or Stanislav Petrov, who chose to defy orders and suffer the consequences rather than push a button and start a nuclear war. And let's not forget Terry Fox, who set out to free the world of cancer one mile at a time. For the sake of others, these people were willing to give up something of themselves — comfort, freedom, personal ambition.

Some people in this book were prepared to pay the ultimate price to help others. Seeing his friend being attacked, Eric Fortier stepped forward to draw the polar bear's attention to himself. Irena Sendlerowa slipped into the Warsaw Ghetto and faced torture and execution to rescue thousands of helpless children. Others like Paul Rusesabagina, Vince Coleman, Anatoly Grischenko, Hellmuth Szprycer, and the Flight 93 passengers and crew knew the risks they were taking, yet they took bold action, putting their own lives on the line to ensure the safety of others.

Some of these people have been called "heroes," yet for a number of them it is an uncomfortable title. "I don't feel like I did something spectacular; I just saw someone who needed help," Wesley Autrey told reporters. "I did what I felt was right." But other people were on the subway platform the day Cameron Hollopeter teetered over the edge. No one else jumped onto the tracks, tackled Cameron, covered him, and narrowly missed being flattened by the subway car. Just Wesley. Why *him*?

Studies of people who take action for the sake of others show that they have a highly tuned sense of empathy.

They are able to put themselves in the shoes of another person, feel what that person feels, think what that person thinks. When situations arise that demand action—a subway train barreling down on a young man, for example—their systems kick into empathy mode: That person needs help. It's up to me. I have to do something.

For some, the call is loud and insistent. There's no second guessing. For these people, to help—whatever the cost—is the right thing to do.

The good news, science tells us, is that empathy is largely a learned attribute. We learn to empathize through examples of care and support given to us at home and school, and through the acts of kindness, generosity, and friendship that we experience.

We learn empathy, too, through stories such as the ones in this book. When we read about great deeds, about acts of courage, determination, and compassion, a little of the story rubs off on us. We gain knowledge and understanding of different situations. Our capacity for empathy deepens, our moral compass realigns, and the hero inside stretches and stirs. There's hope then that if and when *we* are called to action, we will know exactly what we must do.

ACKNOWLEDGMENTS

Many people have helped with this book. I am indebted first and foremost to those whose stories appear on these pages. In the face of great obstacles, each person in this book made difficult decisions, took risks, and demonstrated the power of single-minded action in times of overwhelming need. For their stories of courage and character, I am grateful.

A number of people deserve special mention, among them Andrew Brash and Michael Mayen, who spoke at length about their situations. Thank you for sharing insights that helped to sharpen the book's focus. I am indebted as well to Marie Campbell, my agent for this project, and to the team at Scholastic Canada Ltd.: to Director of Publishing Diane Kerner and senior editor Sandy Bogart Johnston, who saw promise in the initial idea and nurtured it to life; to editor Carrie Gleason, who sifted through my words, checked facts, acquired photographs, asked all-important questions, and kept an open mind to my answers throughout the long process; to designer Aldo Fierro, who gave the manuscript visual impact — my thanks to all.

Finally, I am grateful to my network of support, to friends and family who showed interest, offered suggestions, and encouraged me — my thanks to each of you.

FURTHER READING

Dowswell, Paul. (1996). *Usborne Book of Escape, Survival and Heroism: Tales of Real Adventure*. London: Usborne Publishing Ltd.

Durkee, Coulter (ed). (2006). *Amazing Stories of Survival: Tales of Hope, Heroism & Astounding Luck*. New York: People Books, Time, Inc.

Gonzales, Laurence. (2005). *Deep Survival: Who Lives, Who Dies, and Why*. New York: W.W. Norton & Company.

Nemat, Marina. (2007). *Prisoner of Tehran: A Memoir*. Toronto: Penguin Canada.

Oliner, Samuel. (2004). *Do Unto Others: Extraordinary Acts of Ordinary People*. New York: Perseus Publishing.

Rusesabagina, Paul & Zoellner, Tom. (2006). *An Ordinary Man: An Autobiography*. London: Penguin.

Simpson, Joe. (1988). *Touching the Void: The True Story of One Man's Miraculous Survival*. New York: HarperCollins Publishers.

Yates, Simon. (1998). *Against the Wall*. New York: Vintage Books.

PHOTO CREDITS

MORE BOOKS BY LARRY VERSTRAETE

A former science teacher, Larry Verstraete is the author of a number of books for young readers. His most recent titles are *Lost Treasures,* winner of the McNally Robinson Books for Young People Award and shortlisted for the Hackmatack Award, and *Survivors! True Death-Defying Escapes,* winner of the Silver Birch Award and shortlisted for the Red Cedar Award. His other books include *Extreme Science, Whose Bright Idea Was It?* and *Accidental Discoveries.*

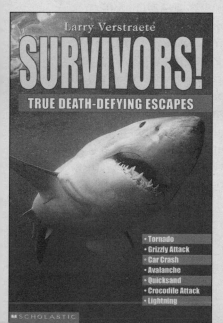

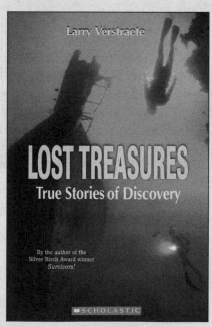